Eye of the Angel

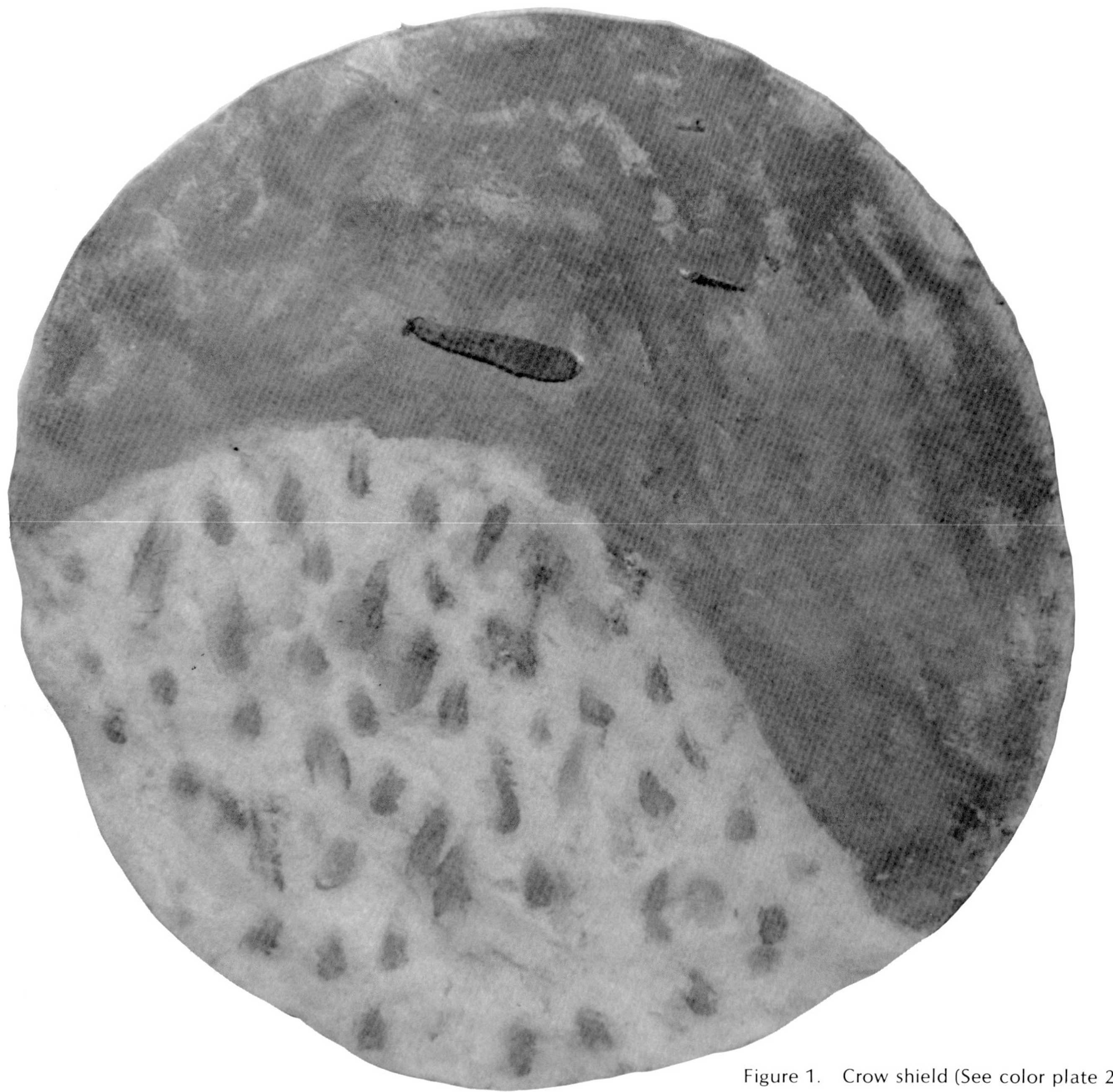

Figure 1. Crow shield (See color plate 28)

Eye of the Angel

Selections from the Derby Collection

Edited by David Wooley

Essays by:

Jonathan Batkin
Robert Bauver
Ted J. Brasser
Charles Derby
John M. Gogol
Benson L. Lanford
F. Dennis Lessard
Richard Pohrt Jr.
Sarah Peabody Turnbaugh
Ruth Holmes Whitehead
David Wooley

WHITE STAR PRESS
P.O. BOX 1268, NORTHAMPTON, MA 01061

White Star Press
P.O. Box 1268
Northampton, MA 01061

Library of Congress catalogue card No. 90-070636

ISBN 0-9626131-O-X

Design: Charles Derby

Mechanical production: Poul Friis-Hansen

Printed in Worcester, Massachusetts by Mercantile Printing Company

On the front of the cover:
Octopus bag
(see essay by Ted J. Brasser)

Photographic Credits:
Cover and color plates 7, 10, 16, 18 by Stephen Petegorsky; color plate 1 by by Manu Sassonian (courtesy of John Molloy); color plates 4, 5, 6, 9, 13, 14, 15, 17, 19, 25, 28 and 29 by Brian Coughlin; color plates 2, 3, 8, 11, 12, 20, 21, 22, 23, 24, 26 and 27 by Charles Derby. All black and white photography by Charles Derby. Black and white processing by Charles Derby and Blanche (Cybèle) Derby. Color processing by Northampton Photographics, Northampton, Massachusetts and COM Color, Springfield, Massachusetts.

Contents

Dedication

To my Grandmother

Carrie Derby

and

To all the Native American Artists

whose work appears in this book

Acknowledgments

Many people have contributed their special knowledge and skill to the realization of this book. A thank you is due first and foremost to David Wooley for taking on the important task of editor. Also I wish to express my sincere thanks to John M. Gogol, for editorial assistance in the basketry area; Doug Deihl, for editorial assistance in the Plains area; and Robert Bauver for editorial assistance in the area of Southwestern pottery. The book owes a great deal to those scholars who contributed essays: F. Dennis Lessard, Richard Pohrt Jr., Sarah Peabody Turnbaugh, Ruth Holmes Whitehead, John M. Gogol, David Wooley, Robert Bauver and Jonathan Batkin. A very special word of thanks to Ted J. Brasser for being the first scholar to agree to participate in this project and for generously giving his encouragement and expertise. I would like to acknowledge Benson L. Lanford and express my profound gratitude to him for all the extra research and writing he did in connection with this book.

I wish to thank Catherine M. Mayhew, society genealogist for the Dukes County Historical Society, for the information she provided about my family history on Martha's Vineyard Island. Many thanks to Elise Bernier-Feeley, Reference Librarian at the Forbes Library, for her assistance. I also want to thank Carl Masthay for providing me with advice on how to write the Indian words which appear in the introduction. In particular I would like to thank my friends Don and Sue Grant and my wife, Cybèle for reading my introductory essay and offering their comments and suggestions. Thanks also to Missy Shea for her secretarial skills in typing many of the essays.

I wish to express my sincere thanks to Marvin Cohodas for identifying some of the baskets in the collection as well as countless other scholars and collectors who may have contributed to my knowledge and understanding. Also I wish to express my appreciation to all the dealers in Indian Art who have worked with me over the years. A very special word of thanks to Jimmy Hart and John Molloy for continuing to offer me beautiful objects which they could have easily sold elsewhere.

Thanks also to Stephen Petegorsky and Brian Coughlin for their help in photography. I would like to express my gratitude to Gary Gurwitz and the staff at Mercantile Printing Company. A special word of thanks to my good friend, Gerry Biron, for all his advice and for allowing me to include his artwork in the book. I wish to thank David Bourbeau for sharing with me his extensive knowledge of books.

Finally, my deepest appreciation to Cybèle for helping me with so many different aspects of the book and to my two sons, Salem and Elias, for being so patient with their dad.

Essays

Contributors' Profiles

Ted J. Brasser is Plains Ethnologist with the Canadian Ethnology Service, Canadian Museum of Civilization, National Museums of Canada, Ottawa.

Sarah Peabody Turnbaugh, M.S., is Curator of the Museum of Primitive Art and Culture in Peace Dale, Rhode Island, and adjunct Assistant Professor of Anthropology at the University of Rhode Island. A major research interest is the study of Native American basketry, a topic on which she has focused for the past two decades.

Ruth Holmes Whitehead is curatorial assistant in History at the Nova Scotia Museum, Halifax, Nova Scotia, Canada.

Richard Pohrt Jr. lives in Ann Arbor, Michigan and is a collector of Native American art. A lifetime of exposure to the subject has led to a particular interest in the arts of the Great Lakes Indians.

F. Dennis Lessard has been a student of American Indian art and culture for over 35 years. He has lectured extensively on various aspects of Indian art and has authored numerous articles on Plains, Prairie and Woodlands arts. He lived for 25 years on the Rosebud Sioux Indian reservation in South Dakota and is now the Director of the Chandler Institute, an ethnographic research center, in Santa Fe, New Mexico.

John M. Gogol is editor and publisher of *American Indian Basketry and Other Native Arts* magazine, and co-editor and publisher of *Mr. Cognito* literary magazine and Mr. Cognito Press. He taught foreign languages (German and Russian) and comparative literature at Pacific University, Colorado State University, and University of Washington.

Benson L. Lanford has been a consultant for a number of museums and private collections. He has lectured extensively and has assisted with the coordination of several American Indian art exhibits.

Jonathan Batkin is Director of The Wheelwright Museum of The American Indian in Santa Fe, New Mexico. He was formerly Co-Director and Chief Curator of The Southwest Museum, Los Angeles, and Curator of The Taylor Museum of The Colorado Springs Fine Arts Center. Batkin has published widely on Native American arts and is author of *Pottery of The Pueblos of New Mexico, 1700-1940* (Colorado Springs, 1987).

David Wooley is curator of The Plains Art Museum, Moorhead, Minnesota.

Robert Bauver is an avid collector of American Indian Art with a special interest in pottery and silverwork. An active art dealer, he exhibits at major shows throughout the United States.

Introduction

Charles Derby

"Two roads diverged in a wood, and I
I took the one less traveled by
and that has made all the difference."
The Road Not Taken by Robert Frost

I am a collector. In fact I've collected for as far back as I can remember; I still have a cast iron fire truck with old red paint which I dug up in the sandbox of my nursery school. As a child I filled my room with rocks, stamps, toy trains, records, baseball cards and comic books, arranging, organizing and cataloging them in a way which may have made sense only to me. I see my five-year-old son, Elias, doing much the same thing with his toys now.

Why collect American Indian Art? I'm sure one of the most important reasons why I got involved was my family background. My great-grandmother, Ana Elizabeth (Manning) Nevers lived in the Native American community of Gay Head on the island of Martha's Vineyard, Massachusetts. She was listed on the census of 1870 as the wife of Daniel Nevers, a seaman twenty-four years her senior. They were listed as having three children. Sometime between 1878 and 1880, Daniel Nevers was lost at sea while serving on a whaling vessel. After that happened, my great-grandmother met and began to live with John P. Ritscher who was working at the Crocker Harness Co. in Vineyard Haven. It is most likely they lived in apartments which were provided by the harness company for their employees. My grandmother, Caroline, was born in 1881 and her sister, Linda, came along two years later.

In the early 1890s my great-grandmother moved to Concord Junction, Massachusetts with her two youngest daughters, Carrie and Linda. She managed a boarding house near the center of town. My grandmother, Carrie, attended Concord Schools and developed her exceptional musical talent by playing the piano each evening for the paying guests.

She met and married Benjamin Derby Jr., the only son of the Derby family—one of the oldest families in the town. They had farmed the same piece of land in Concord since about 1700. I remember my father mentioning that the old Derby farm kitchen had been decorated with weapons which had been given to the family by Indians who worked on the farm in the eighteenth century. My grandfather built a Victorian-style home next to the old farmhouse for his beautiful Indian bride. They had six children and lived a life of relative ease. My grandfather was Postmaster of Concord Junction and also ran a successful business dealing in cattle. During the Depression, however, many people who had purchased cattle on credit were unable to pay. That, coupled with a dispute with his two sisters, Sarah and Anne, led to his financial ruin. He died shortly thereafter.

Meanwhile his sisters had adopted a baby that had been left on the Derby Farm doorstep by a prostitute who had come to Concord Junction from Boston in order to give birth in a place where no one knew her. This foundling ultimately inherited the Derby properties. As a young woman, she opened an antique shop in the barn of the Derby Homestead. She sold the contents of the house which included many early pieces of furniture made by my ancestors as well as the Indian artifacts which had hung on the kitchen walls for so many generations. I remember my grandmother saying in jest that she would have been lucky to even get a rat turd from the Derby Estate.

My grandmother, Carrie, had been raising six children and also developing careers in modeling and singing. She was the first woman to sing on Boston radio, but was best known for her programs of American Indian songs which she performed around New England. She was saved from financial ruin and the loss of her home in Concord by a kind and wealthy relative who gave her the money to purchase a farm in Acton, Massachusetts. My parents joined her on the farm and I was born shortly thereafter.

My childhood was special because I was so close to my grandmother that it seemed as though I had two mothers. Many years earlier, while still in Concord, one of my grandmother's little boys, Robert (her favorite because he looked like an Indian), died in her arms as a result of a childhood accident. She told me that she had visited a psychic after his death and had been told that in the future another little boy would come along for her to love and cherish. She was convinced that I was that little boy described so many years earlier.

As a child I would often crawl into my grandmother's bed to listen to her wonderful stories. Often she would talk about her childhood on Martha's Vineyard Island. She told me about going down to the docks in Vineyard Haven with an old needle, some string and bread. She would catch flounder and bring them home for supper. She also spoke of an old Indian relative who would come from Gay Head on his horse and buggy and take her for rides across the Island. He still spoke /Wampanoag/ and would say to the horses to get them going—/Wiškamíyaha kanča kanča/.

Not all the stories were happy ones. She experienced her share of prejudice as a dark-skinned half-breed in white New England in the late 1800s, like the time the white children refused to let her go sledding on the same hill with them. But she was always proud of her Native American roots and taught me to feel the same way.

One summer in the late 60s while working near Cape Cod, Massachusetts, my friends and I decided, on a whim, to attend a nearby auction. Since I had never been to one before, I didn't know what to expect. In a tiny Grange Hall in Carver, Auctioneer C. L. Norton, his family and friends orchestrated a most memorable evening. Their "Saturday Night Live" auction was part circus and part comedy act, containing some strange and unusual antique offerings. A large Royal Doulton punch bowl covered with portraits of Indian chiefs and sayings from Longfellow's *Hiawatha* still dominates my livingroom—a relic of those wonderful evenings with Clint Norton.

Those auctions were so captivating that I began attending other auctions throughout New England. One fall day I attended a sale run by Ray Murphy and Bill Hubbard at a farm on top of a high hill in Haydenville, Massachusetts. Two American Indian baskets (one inside the other) came up for bid. Even though they were identified as Indian baskets, I was able to buy them for nine dollars. I hurried to the library and found a book by Otis T. Mason called *American Indian Basketry*. In it I found photos of similar baskets to the ones I had just purchased. It was a shock to realize that I could find authentic American Indian objects within my modest price range. For the first time in my life I became truly excited by learning.

A few years after I started collecting and became known in the New England area as an American Indian enthusiast, I met a man from Westport, Connecticut. Paul Rabut tapped me on the shoulder at a Skinner auction preview. He introduced himself and told me he had heard about me and my interest in collecting Indian items. He dropped by to visit on his way home from the sale. We soon began going to auctions and antique shows together on a regular basis and our friendship grew stronger. I had never met anyone—nor have I since—who was as passionately interested in Tribal Art as he was.

One lesson Paul taught me was the value of trading. I simply didn't know that collectors often traded with one another in order to get rare and unusual pieces that they probably couldn't afford to purchase. I remember my first few trades were fraught with worry about whether I was doing the right thing. Soon the simple trades turned into complex deals of several items at a time. Paul and I would often stay up half the night talking about a deal. We would test one another with preposterous suggestions and the entire process became a wonderful game we both enjoyed tremendously.

Paul coined the phrase "Eye of the Angel" to explain how some collectors had an uncanny ability to perceive the very highest level of quality within their area of collecting. Is it instinct? Is one born with it? I'm not sure. I'm reminded of an essay I read years ago by the famous French Tribal Art dealer, Charles Ratton. He mentioned how once in a great while he would meet an unknown collector, living in a very unlikely spot, who would have a remarkably beautiful collection. How did that person acquire such taste? To me "Eye of the Angel" also refers to the special spiritual connection Native American artists have with their work. I hope this book will honor them as well.

In 1975 Richard Stone, a well-known antique jewelry dealer, suggested that I rent a vacant store near his on Green Street in Northampton, Massachusetts. That's how White Star Gallery, specializing in Tribal Art, came to be. In the beginning my inventory was meager but it grew to the point where artifacts were hanging from every possible spot.

About the same time, I started the First Annual New England Antique American Indian Art Show and Sale. I was amazed at the long lines of people from all over the country who came to the show. You could buy a great pair of moccasins for fifty dollars or the best piece in the show—a 26″ high Apache Olla in perfect condition—for sixteen hundred dollars. In the nine years that I ran the show I saw many rare and beautiful Indian Artifacts exchange hands. Eventually the dealers attending the show requested that I move it to a large city. I chose to close the show rather than complicate my life by such a move. When my friend Paul died I reevaluated my goals and decided to close White Star Gallery—dealing in Indian Art wasn't as much fun any more.

Indian baskets were an area of special interest for me early in my collecting. I often went to flea markets looking for them. One of my favorites was acquired on an early morning visit to Brimfield flea market. It was about 7:00 a.m. and I found myself in a quiet section of the field which had opened the previous day. While I was talking to a friend, antique dealers up and down the aisle were putting out their wares for the day's sale. Nearby a large Maidu coiled basket was placed on a table. I walked over and examined it. The price was three hundred and sixty dollars, which was more than I could afford at the time. I put it down and began to walk away. People were cooking breakfast and the smell of bacon drifted in the air. I could hear the voice of a used car salesman on the radio claiming that "no reasonable offer would be refused." Those words caught my attention. I immediately turned around and headed back to take another look at the basket. I had a newfound confidence that I would be able to buy it. The antique dealer was holding the basket as I approached and said "make me an offer." I said "I'll give you two hundred dollars" and he said "It's yours."

As I continued to collect, I was unable to find the books I needed at the local libraries. I, therefore, began to build my own library. I remember reading about the Ghost Dance movement which was begun around 1889 by Wovoka, a Paiute from Nevada. Frequently Ghost Dance believers would go into a trance while dancing and receive instructions for designing their shirts, the most important part of their costume. These shirts, covered with stars, the moon and sacred birds, really appealed to me, so much so that I asked my wife to make me one. I still wear that beautiful shirt on special occasions.

You can imagine my surprise when several years later I saw a real Ghost Dance piece show up at a Massachusetts flea market. It was apparently hanging out of an antique dealer's old laundry basket as she was setting up for the show. It was purchased by a knowledgeable dealer from New Jersey. I saw him shortly after he had acquired it and he was shaking with excitement. He invited me back to his van to get a closer look. When I saw it lying on the grass I fell in love with it. At the time I was not in a position to purchase the piece but I suggested that I was willing to trade. The next day he and his partner came to my home. When they left two hours later, with numerous pieces from my collection, the Ghost Dance cape was mine.

There is an old tag attached to the cape (color plate 18) which says: "Arapaho, $6.00." The cape appears to have been painted by the same person

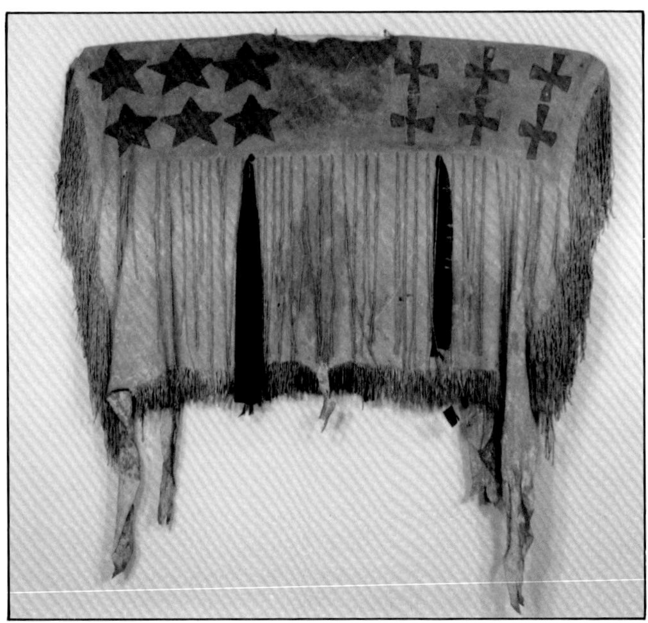

Figure 2. Back of Ghost Dance cape (See color plate 18 for front)

that painted the Arapaho dress in the Chandler-Pohrt Collection which is illustrated on the cover of *I Wear The Morning Star.* It resembles in cut and style an Apache puberty cape. It is not inconceivable that it was made by the Kiowa Apache, or even a more western Apache group, and then ended up among the Arapaho where it was painted. Experiences like this eventually brought a focus to my collecting of American Indian Art. I was not aware that I could collect objects that were not only beautiful but of religious significance. Plains Indian pieces made between 1850 and 1875—the period just before the Indians were placed on reservations—seemed like the perfect choice, blending the aesthetic and the spiritual.

Sometimes Lady Luck smiles upon us when we least expect her blessing. There is a weekly flea market in my area which is located at an abandoned mall. I do not attend on a regular basis, as many do, because I've always thought the odds of finding an Indian item in the booths containing piles of new socks, army surplus jackets and paper flowers is pretty remote. Several years ago, one Sunday just before Christmas, I drove there to search for a book as a gift for an old friend who was visiting for the holidays. I had found what I was looking for and was about to leave when I noticed a used furniture dealer—a late arrival—wheeling his wares into the show on a rickety old handcart. I spied what appeared to be a Navajo rug draped over his pile of oak furniture. I ran over and asked him if it was for sale. I knew immediately it was an exceptional Germantown Chief's Blanket. When he told me it was forty-five dollars, I didn't want to take a chance of unrolling it in front of so many people for fear it would attract attention. When I checked my wallet I found that I was short of cash. My heart nearly jumped out of my chest as I asked him if he would accept a check. He said yes. I still don't know how I wrote it, my hand was shaking so hard. Finally, I threw the blanket over my shoulder and rushed to my car as fast as I could before he changed his mind.

I also believe we make our own luck by listening to our dreams. When I first started advertising in New England antique newspapers my ads were commonplace, yielding little response. One night, in a dream, I saw myself in an advertisement holding an Indian item. When I awoke it seemed like a really good idea to let people see who they were dealing with. My "Familiar Face" ad was born that night and has been extremely successful over the years.

My world of collecting American Indian Art has changed dramatically over the last few years. Most of the collectors that I knew when I began have either died, sold out to corporate interests, or have started collecting in other areas. As prices rise and investors and speculators flock to the marketplace, it is simply more difficult to play the game by the old rules. Recently at a New England auction, I was unsuccessful when I attempted to acquire a new piece for my collection—even though I was willing to pay quite a bit more than I thought it was worth. A few weeks later, an antique newspaper reported that the object was purchased by an investment banker from Boston. I don't like the changes but I do accept them. This book is my way of dealing with them. My deepest wish is that Indian enthusiasts will enjoy reading about my collection as much as I enjoyed putting it together.

A Unique "Indian" Shirt

Ted J. Brasser

Auctioned at Christie's in London in 1986 were a number of Canadian Indian garments, bags, and pouches that had been found in a trunk at Glenbarr Abbey, Scotland. There was no information indicating the origin or history of these objects, except for an old label attached to a skin shirt. This label read: "Hunting dress purchased from Mohawk Indians by the late Hon. John Hope." This John Hope has not been identified, and the shirt is definitely not of Mohawk origin. Materials, shape, and decoration identify it as originating from the northwestern Plains in the first half of the nineteenth century. The same origin and age applies to some of the other items, though there were also some pouches and leggings that appear to have come from a more northern origin at a later date.

There was also another shirt which is now in the Derby Collection. At first glance, this shirt, too, appears to be of northern Plains origin, but there are a number of details that make it a strange and unique garment. Strange is that the skins used in the shirt's manufacture show the many scars made by warble fly larvae. This is a characteristic for skins from the Sub-arctic, never seen on skins from the Plains. Unusual is also the manner in which this shirt has been put together. The body has its poncho style in common with Plains Indian shirts, but the front, with a length of 91 cm., is 35 cm. shorter than the back. Instead of being sewn together on the shoulders, these two skins are attached to a separate shoulder part or yoke, and also the two sleeves have been sewn on to this yoke. A profusion of short and very long fringes were cut from separate pieces and sewn on along sleeves, neck opening, and body. All sewing was done with commercial cotton thread.

The decoration of this shirt is equally unusual. A close inspection of the strange red, white, and blue patterns shows that they were not painted, but stamped with a number of geometric stamps. By means of these stamps, large radiating ornaments were created on the body of the shirt, stars on the shoulders, and stripes on the sleeves. Partially covering these patterns, red cloth panels have been sewn on from the neckline down; these panels are decorated with floral patterns embroidered with dyed moosehair.

Figure 3. Back of Mohawk type shirt (See color plate 1 for front)

This shirt is unique; nothing like it is known from any American Indian collection. But precisely because of this unique character, we may safely assume that it is not one of the clever frauds that have come on the market in recent years. A Canadian origin is most likely, in view of the northern skins of the shirt, its hair-embroidered decoration, and the origin of the other items in the Glenbarr Abbey trunk. The initial impression of seeing a Plains Indian shirt may be significant; it is possible that the shirt's maker had a Plains type in mind but lacked a detailed knowledge of its cut.

Most unusual are the stamped decorative patterns. These patterns also suggest an effort to create something reminiscent of Plains Indian art, the circular pattern of radiating feather designs painted on buffalo robes, and the battle stripes painted on Indian shirts. However, the result of this inspiration is a far cry from native paintings. Moreover, the patterns on this shirt were not painted but stamped.

As far as known to this author, the only recording of stamped decorations on native garments in historic times is to be found in a publication by Frank Speck, dealing with block-stamp decoration on splint basketry in the north-eastern parts of this continent (Speck, 1947:26). Among the Algonquin Indians in Quebec, Speck met an elderly woman who had decorated skin garments with stamped designs. Speck saw this as an adaptation of the stamps that were used to decorate the baskets made by these people as well as by the Mohawk Iroquois along the St. Lawrence River. The manufacture of stamp-decorated splint basketry was adopted by the Algonquins while they were living with these Mohawks until 1854. It is not clear whether the stamp-decoration of skin garments was an independent innovation of the forementioned Algonquin woman, or whether she copied something that she had seen or heard of before.

A second look at the hair-embroidered panels may be useful here. Floral hair embroidery is often attributed to the Huron Indians living near Quebec City in the 1840s. However, the style of the floral patterns on these panels is much more reminiscent of the embossed embroidery of the Mohawks living higher up the St. Lawrence near Montreal. Is it possible that this shirt was made by these Mohawks, who decorated it with their embroidery and an adaptation of their stamped basket decorations?

If anywhere in eastern Canada, it was among these Mohawks in the mid-nineteenth century that there were a number of people acquainted with Plains Indians and their customs. Many of these Mohawks had been employed by the Northwest Company to paddle the flottilas of canoes, leaving Montreal on their annual trips to the far western fur-trading posts of this company. By 1790, there were already Mohawks as free trappers near present Edmonton, Alberta. They were also among the brigades of trappers and traders sent by the Northwest Company to pursue the fur trade west of the Rocky Mountains in 1816. In subsequent years, Mohawk colonies were establiashed on the headwaters of the Saskatchewan River, at the Yellowhead Pass in the Rocky Mountains, and in the region of the Columbia River. Most of these Iroquois were ultimately absorbed by the Metis and local Indian tribes, but others returned to their villages in eastern Canada.

One of them was Thomas Williams, known among his own people as "Two Suns Side By Side." In 1801, he had joined a group of Mohawk trappers on a trip to the Rocky Mountains. Upon his return, he became a chief at St. Regis, a Mohawk settlement on the St. Lawrence River, where he died in 1849 (Hough, 1853:200-203. Frisch, 1978:546). Did he make himself a western style shirt, decorated with "two suns side by side"? But why would he, or any other Mohawk, make himself such a garment?

By 1800 none of these Indians any longer wore skin garments. Trade cloth and European-style garments had been adopted, together with economic occupations related to the needs in the surrounding Canadian society. Many of the local Indians had found work as raftsmen or lumber-jacks, while their women produced large numbers of moccasins and splint baskets for sale. Selling this craftwork, native families roamed the countryside or set up their booths in Montreal and other places frequented by sightseers.

Profiting from the slowly emerging tourist industry, these Mohawks undoubtedly soon discovered that a 'real Indian' appearance paid off. This is the most likely motivation for the manufacture of a garment like this shirt. Admittedly it is by means of mere circumstantial evidence that I suggest that this shirt was made by a Mohawk Indian in the early decades of the nineteenth century—a man in need of an 'Indian' garment, utilizing his memory of Plains Indian fashions as well as decoration techniques of his own people. This conclusion would also account for the label, referring to the Mohawk Indians, later by mistake attached to another shirt in the Glenbarr Abbey trunk.

From the Top of Her Head: The Woman's Dress Cap of Northwestern California

Sarah Peabody Turnbaugh

Many small villages of the Karuk, Yurok, Hupa, and neighboring tribes once were located in northwestern California, in the rugged valleys along the rushing Klamath and Trinity rivers and their tributaries in the deep canyons and steep, forested ridges of Del Norte and northern Humboldt counties. There, hunter-gatherers stalked elk and deer and fished for salmon, trout, and lamprey eels, in addition to relying on acorns and other gathered foodstuffs for their subsistence (Goddard 1903:21-22). Today, remnant native populations of these peoples live primarily on Hoopa Valley Reservation, where they have retained their traditional languages and lifeways to a limited extent, despite considerable cultural intermixture (Bright 1978).

Although similar in many ways to other ethnic groups of northern California, the Karuk, Yurok, Hupa, and several neighboring groups were geographically, linguistically, and culturally isolated. They seldom interacted with native peoples located outside of their region (O'Neale 1932:143). However, the groups residing in the vicinity of the Klamath and Trinity rivers lived in close contact, frequently intermarrying, trading, and visiting among themselves (O'Neale 1932:138).

Despite completely different linguistic and cultural origins of the Karuk, Yurok, and Hupa, their nineteenth-century social organization and material culture was similar. Basketry was their most highly developed technology. Nineteenth- to early twentieth-century examples from each ethnic group closely resemble each other (Kroeber 1905:106), though minor distinctions in each group's technology, form, materials, and choice of color and design elements and layouts are evident (O'Neale 1932; Turnbaugh and Turnbaugh 1986:176-181).

The Karuk, Yurok, and Hupa structured their basketry designs in similar ways. In an extensive reanalysis of Lila O'Neale's ethnographic data, Dorothy Washburn (1978, personal communication) found that the predominant group of

Figure 4. Woman's dress cap (See color plate 2)

Plain twined cap with half-twist overlay decoration in white beargrass, black maidenhair fern, and yellow (tree lichen?) dyed porcupine quills. The design field of the cap is divided into three traditional design bands. In the first band at the top center of the cap, the start or "button" is overlaid with yellow-dyed quill. It is surrounded by a circle of black maidenhair fern overlay, then by a ring of brown three-strand twining; then a black maidenhair fern circle; a yellow-dyed quill circle; a black and yellow design band that the Karuk call "kutsisivac" or "spotted" (Kroeber 1905: 132, 141); and a white beargrass circle. The central or main design band is bordered at both top and bottom with narrow black and yellow circles of the "kutsisivac" design element. The Karuk named the prominent black and yellow design element in the center of the white field "apxankoikoi" or "friendship" (Kroeber 1905: 129, 131, 141). The third band, located at the rim of the cap, is white with black and yellow triangular design elements, called "apcuniu'fi" or "snake-nose" (Kroeber 1905: 131, 141) in Karuk. The simple rim finish consists of clipped-off willow warp elements.

Late 19th century. Collection data supplied to Charles Derby by the former owner are sketchy but indicate the cap was collected in California, ca. 1880s, and is Karuk. Rim diameter = 18.5 cm.; height = 10.5 cm.; twined rows/cm. = 7; stitches/cm. = 7.

structured designs correlated exactly with those baskets the native weavers told O'Neale were "good." The miscellaneous designs with different structures correlated with those O'Neale's informants said were "bad" or not "proper" designs. Washburn demonstrated that design structure is a sensitive indicator of group consensus, or of a similar cultural identity, for these people. Further analysis of baskets created by surrounding groups with whom the Karuk, Yurok, and Hupa did not interact as much revealed markedly different design structures. Comparable studies (e.g., Turnbaugh 1977, Turnbaugh and Turnbaugh 1987) for attributes of basketry technology, form, design, and materials have demonstrated similar correlations through time and over space for other cultural groups elsewhere in North America.

This writer has yet to locate a second example of a button overlaid with yellow-dyed quill. Marcy L. Burns (1989, personal communication to Derby), however, mentioned that the start in quill is something that she would associate with Hickox's baskets. From an anthropological point of view, perhaps the *quill* overlaid button was contextually important; one of J. P. Harrington's informants, the dealer E. G. Johnson, suggested that, "Any cap with yellow porcupine quill in it is a wedding cap" (Eisenhart 1981: Fig. 97b caption). Possibly the technology of the Derby cap reflects an intended specific, contextual use. Or, perhaps the quill overlaid button was created due to a weaver's personal fondness for the material or color, difficult as it was to prepare the quills and execute the quill overlay. The Karuk weaver Elizabeth Hickox (born 1873) was the daughter of a Wiyot woman and seems to have had a particular fondness for using yellow-dyed porcupine quills. She occasionally made baskets decorated all over with quills (Eisenhart 1981:36). A quill-covered trinket basket by Hickox, for example, is housed at the Riverside Municipal Museum (Martha Spark 1990, personal communication). When J. P. Harrington questioned Hickox about her preference, Hickox indicated that it was "the old way" (to make baskets covered with porcupine quills). One of Harrington's main informants, Karuk basketmaker Phoebe Maddux, later disagreed. She was emphatic that Mrs. Hickox was incorrect in calling quill overlay a traditional decorative method, saying, "They never did make them that way. We thought it was so funny when she (Hickox) made them thus" (Eisenhart 1981:36). However, whether or not Hickox or another Karuk weaver ever overlaid buttons with quill is not yet documented. The possibility does, of course, exist that the Derby cap may be of non-Karuk (e.g., Yurok, Wiyot, or Hupa) origin. The use of yellow-dyed quills seems to have been more common generally among Yurok, Wiyot, and Hupa peoples than among the Karuk (O'Neale 1932:23, 60-61). That the Karuk basketmaker Hickox was the daughter of a Wiyot woman and also liked to use yellow-dyed quills cannot be discounted; the fact that Hickox gave up cap making early in her career (Cohodas 1989, personal communication)—perhaps while any maternal Wiyot influence was still strongest for her—also is worthy of consideration.

A second attribute of interest is the even weave and the stitch count for the Derby cap; the average count of twined stitches/cm is 7 and of rows/cm is 7-8. These data demonstrate that the Derby cap is unusually finely woven. A similar cap—which was woven by the Karuk weaver Mrs. Jim Pepper using the "apxankoikoi" element in the main design zone (Eisenhart 1981: Fig. 97b)—is finely woven but averages only 5 stitches/cm. While the "apxankoikoi" element is not one known to have been used by Elizabeth Hickox, as mentioned above, the use of willow warp elements and the unusually even, fine stitch counts are typical of Hickox's work, among that of several others. A basketry cap in the recently accessioned Becker Collection of the Clarke Memorial Museum is attributed to Elizabeth Hickox and has dimensions that are similar to those for the Derby cap: 18.5 cm (dia.); 8.5 cm (h.); 7-8 rows/cm; and 6-7 stitches/cm. Other contemporaries of Hickox also number among the best Karuk weavers and are known for their basketry caps, including Nettie Ruben (mid-1870s–1957), who wove Hover Collection cap #11 (18.0 x 8.7 cm; 7 rows/cm; 5 stitches/cm—the stitches have a somewhat rough, irregular appearance); Elsie McLaughlin (1880-1954), who wove Hover Collection cap #10 (17.0 x 7.2 cm; 7-8 rows/cm; 5-6 stitches/cm—the stitches are very even and regular); and Mrs.

Jim Pepper, who wove a cap (Eisenhart 1981: Fig. 97b) with measurements of 16.5 x 8.5 cm; 5 stitches/cm. The number of stitches/cm and rows/cm generally is not as fine as examples by Hickox, however. Yet, stitch counts often vary and are not diagnostic alone; Hickox's stitches, for example, for Hover Collection #88—a lidded basket—range from 4-6 stitches/cm and from 8-10 rows/cm.

THE DERBY CAP

Given this cultural background as context, the woman's dress cap featured in the Charles Derby Collection will now be considered.

Derby's cap is both correctly and finely executed in terms of criteria important to native northwestern California basketmakers. Choice of twining technologies, materials, color combinations, design elements, and design layout are all precisely correct according to native conventions, described in Kroeber (1905) and detailed in O'Neale (1932:41-100). The cap was made by an accomplished basketmaker, adhering closely to conventions. She chose only the finest materials (for example, yellow-dyed porcupine quills were used only in the best of baskets), and all her choices of materials (Elsasser 1978) were traditionally correct. She selected proper, conventional design elements common to each ethnic group, including "apxankoikoi" for the main design zone. This design element is difficult to execute well because the number of warp elements must correspond precisely (Fields 1985:55; Riverside Municipal Museum 1990:56). While design shifts are visible in the banded "kutsisivac" or "spotted" pattern, no shift is visible in the execution of the central design band "apxankoikoi" of the Derby cap. The Karuk weaver Elizabeth Hickox, among others, mastered the avoidance of warp splices so that patterns would not shift (Richard Conn 1990, personal communication). Lizzie Hickox is not known to have created the "apxankoikoi" design element (Martha Spark 1990, personal communication), though several of her contemporaries, including Nettie Ruben and Mrs. Jim Pepper, did (Eisenhart 1981: Fig. 97b; Fields 1985: 66, Fig. 42).

Only in the area of form did the weaver of the cap diverge somewhat from expected norms. The dimensions of Derby's cap are larger than those for many similar examples of ceremonial caps (cf. Fields 1985:59-63; Turnbaugh and Turnbaugh 1986:174-175), suggesting that it was made for a relatively large-headed woman. Second, Derby's cap proportionally is within range but higher than the average height/diameter ratio that this writer obtained for 35 other Karuk caps, including examples at the Clarke Memorial Museum, Smithsonian Institution, and Peabody Museum of Harvard. This ratio, in the absence of conclusive accession data, is an attribute that suggests that Derby's cap truly is of Karuk origin—rather than a Yurok or Hupa example, which look very similar but tend to be lower proportionally (Harrington 1932:127).

Further analysis of Derby's cap reveals two other interesting attributes. The basketry start, or "button," is overlaid with yellow-dyed porcupine quills. Several late nineteenth- to early twentieth-century basketmakers created overlaid buttons. Elizabeth Hickox is known for her buttons overlaid with black maidenhair fern, but she also occasionally overlaid them with white beargrass (Fields 1985:40, 75). Several of her contemporaries including Elsie McLaughlin (1880-1954) also overlaid buttons with beargrass (Fields 1985: Figs. 87, 90).

DISCUSSION

Derby's cap highlights the divergent perspectives of makers of traditional native arts and of modern-day collectors of those arts. Ironically, while the practitioners sought to conform to cultural conventions and to the work of their peers in terms of materials, technology, design, proportion, and form, the collectors of those same objects today doggedly seek the individual native artist, rather than tolerating anonymity.

To be culturally acceptable, northwestern California dress caps adhered to the highest, most rigorous standards of a tradition in which individual expression and artistic license were eschewed. Innovation or variation from cultural rules governing the creation of the cap could attract social disapproval for the maker and rejection of the cap as inappropriate or worthless.

Contemporary collectors of native American arts, themselves generally participants in a society stressing individualism, often have circumvented traditional native systems by seeking out and rewarding the individual artist. The Washo basketmaker Datsolalee and the Karuk basketmaker Elizabeth Hickox serve as cases in point. Both came to the notice of wealthy patrons who commissioned their work and provided remuneration, promotion, and recognition. Modern-day collectors perpetuate this preoccupation with individual identity.

While the actual maker of Derby's cap has not been definitively established in this essay, the exquisite cap clearly was created by one of the most skilled late nineteenth- to early twentieth-century practitioners of the craft. Native basket-makers would count this dress cap among the finest examples of the basketry form—both in terms of its adherence to cultural conventions and in its superlative execution. Any modern-day collector or scholar would agree and would include the cap among the choice examples of native basketry art.

ACKNOWLEDGMENTS

Many people have added to my understanding of native American basketry through the past two decades, and I thank them for helping to increase my cumulative knowledge of the subject. For this project in particular, I thank Marcy L. Burns, Marvin Cohodas, Richard G. Conn, Lawrence Dawson, Charles Derby, and Dorothy Washburn, who provided opinions and personal communications regarding the Derby cap. I am especially grateful to Martha Spark of the Clarke Memorial Museum, California, for her patient assistance in providing stitch/cm and row/cm measurements on several Karuk basketry caps attributed to known makers, for comparison with the Derby example. Finally, I thank my husband, William A. Turnbaugh, for shared conversations about the Derby cap, to which he contributed his own extensive knowledge of native American basketry and anthropological cultural process.

Micmac Porcupine Quillwork in the Derby Collection

Ruth Holmes Whitehead

The Micmac women of eastern Canada were creating exquisite artwork with porcupine quills centuries before contact with the European writers who would begin to document this craft and introduce it to the rest of the world.[1] Multiple techniques of embroidery, weaving, appliqué, wrapping, and twisting of quills added a jewel-like glitter and color to costumes and to surfaces such as snowshoe rims, pipe stems, and shamans' rattles. After 1500 A.D., such quilled items were eagerly sought by fishermen, explorers, fur traders, and settlers coming to North America from the Old World. A favorite was the Micmac tobacco pouch, with its panels of bead-like woven quills and its multiple quill-wrapped fringes.[2] At some point during the first two hundred years of contact, a new form of quillwork rose to prominence: the mosaic of porcupine quills on a foundation of birchbark. The bark was then fashioned into boxes, canoe models, and other shapes calculated to catch a European eye.

Birchbark *(Betula Papyrifera)* is an ideal base for a quill mosaic. A waxy resinous component makes it impervious to water and bacterial attack, insects dislike the taste of it, and it can be cut and shaped while retaining a leathery toughness and flexibility. Birchbark is smooth to the touch, and comes in a variety of shades, from white to cream to fawn, gold, and brown. The bark is warmed and kept damp while being worked, a pattern then scratched on, and holes made in the bark to receive the quill ends. Birchbark has the property of immediately closing small punctures in its surface, so that holes are pierced one at a time, and a single quill end inserted, by which time the bark has contracted tightly around the quill, holding it in place. A second hole is made for the other end of the quill, and the whole process repeated a thousand times, and thus the mosaic is built up. On completion, the protruding quill ends on the reverse of the bark are clipped off.

Quills are also worked wet, for flexibility. Micmac women preferred the long thin back quills from *Erithizon dorsatum,* the Eastern

Figure 5

a. Quillwork box, Micmac type, ca. 1820. H: 15 cm, D: 21 cm

b. Quillwork box, Micmac type, ca. 1800. H: 16 cm, L: 23 cm, W: 18.5 cm

c. Quillwork box, Micmac type, ca. 1800. H: 11 cm, L: 17.5 cm, W: 13 cm

Porcupine. These are white with black tips, the black portion not being included in Micmac designs. Organic dyes for the quills included a russet or red-gold from Bloodroot *(Sanguinaria canadensis),* a pale yellow from Goldthread *(Coptis trifolia),* a black which may have come from Black Spruce bark *(Picea mariana),* a commercially obtained Indigo blue, a flaming red from Red Bedstraw roots *(Galium tinctorium),* and an unknown green, possibly from *Taxus canadensis.*

For sewing together their quilled-bark creations, the Micmac employed the long pale split roots of Black Spruce, which they also used decoratively, both by dyeing the roots and by utilizing them as warps interwoven with white quills, forming checkered patterns on the edges of boxes or bowls. In the late nineteenth century, very small and delicate panels of bark were sometimes seamed to silk ribbon, the other edge of the ribbon then being sewn to another panel of bark.

This new form of bark-insertion quillwork was enlarged and refined into a made-for-trade commodity. Over the following two hundred years, it became both the hallmark craft of the Micmac and a major source of cash-or-barter income. More and more European forms were added to the quillworker's repertoire: jewel boxes and hat cases by 1774,[3] flower pots with attendant saucers by 1830, lampshades, wastepaper baskets, fire screens, firewood caddies, tea cosies, doll cradles, fans, cases for playing cards, calling cards, cigars, spectacles, watches and needles,

Figure 6

a. Quillwork box, Micmac type, ca. 1850. H: 12 cm, L: 23 cm, W: 16 cm

b. Quillwork box, Micmac type, ca. 1850. H: 12.5 cm, L: 18 cm, W: 14.5 cm

c. Quillwork box, Micmac type, ca. 1850. H: 9 cm, L: 14.5 cm, W: 13 cm

portfolios, and ornamental panels for furniture. Nesting sets of boxes, which in turn held other boxes, are reported as early as 1773.[4] The popular furniture panels included chair seats, backs and back splats, or chair arms, as well as panels for the tops of tea tables, with a bare spot left in the center for the hot teapot. Micmac women sometimes created works that covered the entire piece of furniture, such as the unique baby cradle now in the DesBrisay Museum at Bridgewater, N.S. The quilling for this took a year to complete. Quillwork furniture panels were sold to cabinetmakers, who then put together the furniture base for them.

The most ubiquitous form this type of porcupine quillwork took, however, was the lidded box, as represented by the twelve examples in the Derby Collection.[5] Of the many types made over the centuries between 1700 and 1950—when this art died out—the circular box seems to have been both the earliest and most prevalent shape.

Box One (Figure 5a) in the Derby Collection is a typical construction of this type. A circular piece of softwood (older boxes sometimes use bark) forms the base, and is attached with small wooden pegs to the lowest of the three rings that form the sides of the box. (Bark bases are attached with root stitchery.) Such exterior rings are made of birchbark wrapped with spruce root. Here three of them are slipped over the box's plain bark liner, then secured to one another by groups of two spruce-root stitches. The lid side is constructed in the same way and fitted on over the liner projection. Undyed porcupine quills, larger in size than those used to form the lid-top mosaic, are threaded through the spruce-root wrap on box and lid sides, creating small checkered geometric designs.

The lid top to this circular box is of birchbark, sewn with root to the lid side. The root stitches pass over an edging of two lengths of the same root. The central area is quilled in geometric motifs of semicircles, triangles, and rectangular forms, the symbolic meaning of which is now unknown. Some of the interstices between solidly quilled areas have been further decorated with "fill" quilling, using one or two widths of quills. The sparse nature of this fill, and of the secondary "overlay" quill designs indicate a date in the early nineteenth century, approximately 1820-1830. Organic dyes of indigo, russet, and pale yellow support this date, as does the root-wrapping—as opposed to quilling—of the box sides.

Eight of the boxes in the Derby Collection are rectangular, with flat lids, calling for a slightly different method of construction. Again, the bases are of softwood, a rectangle pinned to the box exterior with wooden pegs. The liners, however, are not bark, but four separate wooden pieces—one for each side—with their edges beveled to fit against each other. Liners project above the box sides in order that the lids may be slipped on over them and supported.

Box Two (Figure 5b) has an exterior of three root-wrapped bands of bark decorated with diamond-patterns of interwoven white quills. The lid side is similar, sewn to the lid top with root over a single edging length of root. The quilled design on the lid top is very simple, with minimal fill and no overlay. The central motif is a rectangle composed of four triangles on a russet diamond. An interlock design runs along two interfaces between diamond and rectangle. Further geometric motifs of stepped shapes, triangles, rectangles, and arcs complete the mosaic. Dyes are similar to those in Box One. An approximate date would be 1800-1820.

Box Three (Figure 5c) is made in the same

Figure 7

a. Quillwork box, Micmac type, ca. 1850. H: 14 cm, L: 21.5 cm, W: 18 cm

b. Quillwork box, Micmac type, ca. 1850. H: 7 cm, L: 11.5 cm, W: 8.5 cm

c. Quillwork box, Micmac type, ca. 1850. H: 10 cm, L: 20.5 cm, W: 15.5 cm

way, but has only two root-wrapped bands making up the exterior. Its interweave is a simple chain-link pattern using three quill-lengths. The lid top is decorated in a truncated half-chevron pattern, common in early nineteenth-century boxes, using organic dyes as above.

Box Four (Figure 6a) is later in date— probably 1850—and immediately several stylistic changes can be noted. The box side now consists of a single wide strip of bark, ornamented with a quill mosaic, such as previously seen only on the box lids. A chevron pattern is used, with a lattice effect of crisscross quills in the interstices of the chevrons. Spruce-root lengths are edged with quilled areas, held on with smaller root stitches.

The lid top, now detached from the lid side and repaired with thread, has a central eight-pointed star motif. One twentieth-century quill-worker referred to this as an Eight-legged Starfish. Earlier records, recently uncovered, show that this symbol was employed by the Micmac to represent the sun. The same eight-pointed star appears as Micmac rock-art, cut with stone tools and thought to be pre-European, at a site near Bedford, N.S.

Box Four's quillwork has a much more elaborate use of fill, interlock, and overlay quilling. The overlay might even be called fussy. Organic dyes still appear to have been used, with the addition of an oily greenish-black of unknown origin.

Box Five (Figure 6b) has chevron designs on the exterior with white triangles in the interstices. This is by far the most common motif on boxes with quilled sides. The box lid has a central X motif, which divides the box into four triangles. An examination of Box Six (Figure 6c) shows how this X motif has here been divided, with a diamond in the center space. (Note also the red and black dye on the spruce root which wraps the lid-side of Six.) On Box Seven (Figure 7a) the X has shrunk even further, as the diamond has been more heavily emphasized with fill. The lid sides on Box Seven have been quilled rather than wrapped. All three of these boxes appear to date to the mid-nineteenth century.

Box Eight (Figure 7b) is of similar vintage, and has rather endearingly messy quillwork on the lid sides. Note the nice overlay on the lid top. The box is in need of cleaning, but the organic dye-colors seem to include yellow and white, as well as the more obvious russet and blue.

Box Nine (Figure 7c) is more of an anomaly. The diagonal sides—made by staggering the quillwork insertions that form the horizontal stripes—do appear on other Nova Scotian-made pieces from the nineteenth century. An interlocking insertion on the lid top and the use of white space create a strong and unusual design, yet one which is recognizably Micmac, and probably mid-nineteenth century.

Box Ten (Figure 8a) is rectangular, but with a vaulted top. Lid construction of this nature involves a rectangular bark piece for the lid top, bent and sewn to a lid-side of a single band of bark, with the upper edges cut in such a way as to force the top into a trunk-lid shape. Both pieces of bark are quilled. The shiny black, green, and faded red of this box are probably inorganic aniline dyes—available in Canada after 1865.

Boxes Eleven (Figure 8b, Color Plate 3) and Twelve (Figure 8c) are oval or ovate. They take their shapes from their softwood bases. A bark liner is used, as in the circular boxes. Box Eleven is in excellent condition. The central lid-top motif is the eight-pointed star. It was apparently brought back to New England by 1853, from

Figure 8

a. Quillwork box, Micmac type, ca. 1870. H: 13 cm, L: 21 cm, W: 17 cm

b. Quillwork box, Micmac type, ca. 1853. H: 13 cm, Max. D: 27 cm

c. Quillwork box, Micmac type, ca. 1920. H: 9 cm, Max. D. 21.5 cm

Prince Edward Island.[6]

Box Twelve is a more pinched-oval shape, similar examples of which have been noted as coming from the south shore of Nova Scotia, probably made during the 1920s. Overlay quilling catches the eye here more than the actual designs, although dyes have faded, and this box was possibly vividly red and yellow in places.

Because of the many historic ties of kinship and trade between Maritime Canada—ancestral homeland of the Micmac people who made these boxes—and New England, many New England museums and private collections contain quillwork items. Many of these pieces were collected locally. Nineteenth-century ships' captains often traded in these wares as a sideline; travelers and sailors brought such items home as gifts. Box Eleven (Figure 8b, Color Plate 3) contains a note reading, "Porcupine quill oval box brought home from Prince Edward Island in 1853 by grandfather Henry Eagle U.S.N." In addition, a woman from Pictou, N.S.—evidently an ardent abolitionist—is on record as having shipped crates of porcupine quillwork to Boston to be auctioned off to finance the abolitionist cause in the United States.[7] The Derby Collection is an example of the longevity of the fascination with quillwork, as it contains items ranging from 1800 to 1920, and a number of different styles, shapes, and construction methods.

Great Lakes Bandolier Bags In the Derby Collection

Richard Pohrt Jr.

The introduction of certain European trade goods had a dramatic effect upon the artwork of the Great Lakes tribes. Cotton and wool cloth replaced animal hides as clothing material. Glass beads and silk ribbon replaced porcupine quills as preferred decorative mediums. The navy, black, and red cloth that the Indians acquired in trade provided an excellent background for bead and ribbon ornamentation. In fact, the black and navy blue cloth resembled their black buckskin predecessors. Distinctly native objects were fashioned using exclusively European materials. Many of these items (bandolier bags, sashes, garters, skirts, blouses, leggings, yarn bags, hoods, etc.) are artworks of the highest order, demonstrating a creative imagination and original designs and techniques. The Derby Collection contains a number of fine objects from the Great Lakes region. These include a superb Midewiwin otter bag and a number of nice woven beadwork sashes. However, the artistic traditions of the Great Lakes Indians are best exemplified by a fine group of seven woven beadwork bandolier bags. These bags all date from the later half of the nineteenth century. It was during this period that the tribes in the western Great Lakes (Chippewa, Winnebago, Potawatomi, Menomini, Ottawa) produced great quantities of woven beadwork. These people quickly transformed the variously colored hanks of glass seed beads into magnificent objects of personal adornment. The woven bandolier bag represents the apex of the beadworker's art. Four of the Derby bandolier bags have been chosen for illustration. Together, they give us a hint of the variety of designs and color concepts we encounter in woven beadwork. Geometric forms tend to be the dominant motif (Illustrations 1, 3, 4) but foliate patterns also emerge (Illustration 3). Occasionally, human or animal forms occur. The pouch on the bandolier bag illustrated as number 4 contains numerous stylized thunderbirds as the major design element. All colors and shades of beads were used in the making of these bags.

No one is quite sure as to when and how the bandolier bag came into use amongst the Indians of the Great Lakes. There is some speculation that earlier examples were modeled after European shot pouches. They may also have developed from an aboriginal prototype. During the late eighteenth and early nineteenth centuries, bandolier bags evolved from examples on black dyed buckskin with porcupine quill decoration and simple straps to slightly larger examples with finger woven yarn pouches and straps. These bags were decorated by integrating beads into the woven fabric to produce a particular design—often an openwork diamond pattern in white beads. The earliest documented bandolier bags using woven beadwork as ornamentation date from the 1850's. Two particularly well known examples (one at the Nelson Atkins Museum of Art in Kansas City and one belonging to the Detroit Historical Society, Historic Fort Wayne) bear the dates 1850 and 1851, woven into the

Figure 9. Bandolier Bag, Santeaux type, ca. 1877. Red trade cloth; brown and olive binding; cotton print backing; black cotton lining; white, yellow, black, green, red, lavender and medium blue glass beads; red and green wool yarn. 98 cm x 27 cm

beaded panel.[1] These early beaded bags tend to mimic their predecessors in form. They have relatively narrow and short straps and compact pouches. Later examples, such as those illustrated here, tend to exhibit wider and longer straps and larger pouches. Towards the very end of the nineteenth century, bandolier bags underwent further change as the woven beadwork bags were supplanted by appliqué beaded bags decorated with realistic floral motifs. The Derby Collection includes one such example from this final period, but it was not selected for illustration.

As bandolier bags changed stylistically over time, so did their use. Their utilitarian function as a pouch or an extra pocket was abandoned to the extent that by the late nineteenth century, they were worn purely as objects for personal adornment. Numerous period photographs show Indians wearing two bandolier bags as well as extra sashes and garters.[2] A notable number of examples are found without backing and/or without pockets.

Perhaps more importantly, many bandolier bags were made to be offered as gifts, demonstrating the generosity and enhancing the prestige of the giver. The tribes of the western Great Lakes lived in close proximity and on friendly terms in the later half of the nineteenth century. Bandolier bags were distributed as gifts at tribal and intertribal gatherings. Bandolier bags are sometimes referred to as "Friendship Bags," a term that defines their purpose as opposed to method of wearing. Ideas for design and color combinations spread as these bags passed through various Indian hands. This may also have served as an impetus for greater artistic creation.

One bandolier bag has been chosen as color plate six (Figure 9). This bag probably dates to the 1870s and is a classic example from the period. Accurate dating of bandolier bags is complicated by the overlapping of styles and inadequate collection history. Some latitude in dating is usually preferable. However, attention to certain details can encourage more precise dating. The use of red trade cloth for backing (in contrast to the later use of black velveteen), the lack of applied bead decoration to the cloth area above the pouch, the relative dimensions of the bandolier, and even the color and shades of beads, when considered in this combination, suggest the 1870s dating.

The design motifs on the shoulder strap are asymmetrical, a common feature with many of these bags (note Illustrations 3, 4). On one side, the artist has created a complex design by modifying and expanding upon a basic diamond form. On the opposite side, a foliate pattern in yellow beads is predominate along with further variations of the diamond. The pouch repeats the color combinations of the shoulder strap without repeating the designs. Four elaborate X designs dominate the surface, accented again with diamond motifs. The pouch ends with long woven bead fringes that are tied off with red and green yarn tassels. The pouch area is outlined with white seed beads applied directly to the cloth in an openwork diamond pattern. The loom woven strap and pouch are sewn onto a backing of red trade cloth. The shoulder strap is further reinforced with a backing of calico cloth. A sturdy cotton braid is used to edge the entire bag.

This bandolier deserves closer attention because it may have some historic association. The bag was acquired from an auction house. Overlooked in the pouch was an old note card describing the bandolier as an "Indian Pouch or Fire Bag. Made by a squaw of the Santeaux tribe Northwest of Lake Superior. This pouch was worn by one of the chiefs of Joseph's tribe of Nez Perce in the Battle of Bear Paw Mountains, where the band were overcome by Gen. Miles." Like much "documentation," this information can be as confounding as it is illuminating. No one has signed or dated the card, so who do we attribute it to? Did the original collector write it? Did the collector obtain the bag directly from the Nez Perce chief or was this information that had been passed along? Unfortunately, we cannot turn back time and fill in the answers. We can only analyze this information and frame it within the context of what we know (or are more certain about). Santeaux is an archaic term used to refer to some Chippewa, groups of which have resided in the area north and west of Lake Superior since times of earliest contact with whites. Surrounded by United States troops, Chief Joseph was forced to surrender on October 5, 1877, following a remarkable retreat that left him within 50 miles of the Canadian border, the objective point of his band. The making of this bandolier by a "squaw of the Santeaux tribe" seems inarguable. Dating the bag to 1877 is within the time parameters for this style. We can only speculate as to how this bandolier bag traveled from the western Great Lakes to central Montana. Chief Joseph was photographed wearing a Great Lakes bandolier bag in a well-known studio portrait dated circa 1877.[3] There is another photo, this one taken in 1908, of a Nez Perce Indian who has dropped a Winnebago bandolier bag over the neck of his horse.[4] All manner of native items were circulated through intertribal trading networks. So, it is reasonable to accept the likelihood that this bandolier bag did find its way to the Nez Perce.

Any survey of woven beadwork can be a rewarding experience. Highly original design concepts as well as clever variations of common motifs frequently present themselves. The bandolier bags in the Derby Collection give us one more opportunity to marvel at these attractive objects.

A Wicasas Shirt In the Derby Collection

F. Dennis Lessard

The Derby shirt is a classic central Plains two-hide garment made from two whole antelope hides, the front quarters and neck skin of each hide forming the sleeves and the remaining three-quarters of each hide being used for the front and back of the shirt. The leg skin of each hide was retained and appears as appendages on each sleeve and at the lower hem of the shirt front and back. It is a poncho style with the sides being open (or loosely tied) and the sleeves are sewn shut for only 6 inches near the wrist. All edges of the hide are self-fringed except the wrist ends of the sleeves. There is unusually long self-fringing on the bottom hem of the garment. The bib or neck flap is an added U-shaped piece, which is decorated with red trade cloth, lazy-stitch beadwork, and painted buckskin fringes.

The shirt measures 32 inches long, 23 inches wide through the body, and 56 inches wide from sleeve end to sleeve end, a very large garment. The top three-quarters of the shirt is painted a dark royal blue color—a very rich color, undoubtedly a trade pigment, possible laundry bluing. The remainder of the shirt is painted a pale yellow ochre color. (Figure 10)

The porcupine quill shoulder and sleeve strips are bordered with a narrow lane of lazy-stitched beadwork executed in pony-trader-blue seed beads. The quillwork is two-thread, single quill, sewn work, (Figure 11), seven lanes wide, with red and pale blue (perhaps faded dark blue) bar and block patterns against a yellow background. These quilled strips, both on the sleeves and shoulders, are the second set of strips this garment has had, as evidence of previous longer and wider strips remain. The blue paint has been applied to the shirt after the present quilled strips were attached.

A profusion of quill-wrapped human hair locks has been attached to the sleeves along the rear edge of the quilled strips and to the body of the shirt along the outer edge of the quilled shoulder strips on the back of the shirt. The decorated hair fringes—often called "scalp locks"—on the body of the shirt have white quillwork at the top, while those on the sleeves

Figure 10. Front of shirt (See color plate 16 for back)

Figure 11. Schematic drawing of two-thread, single quill, sewn quillwork.

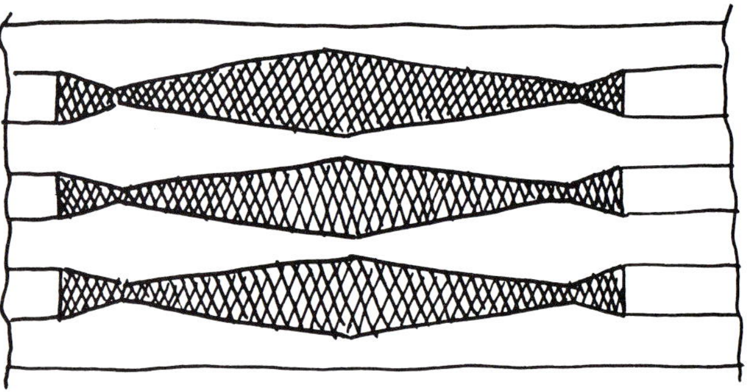

Figure 12. Schematic drawing of a design from an early quilled shirt, ca. 1860.
Read Collection.
Cat. #1881.3.156 LA

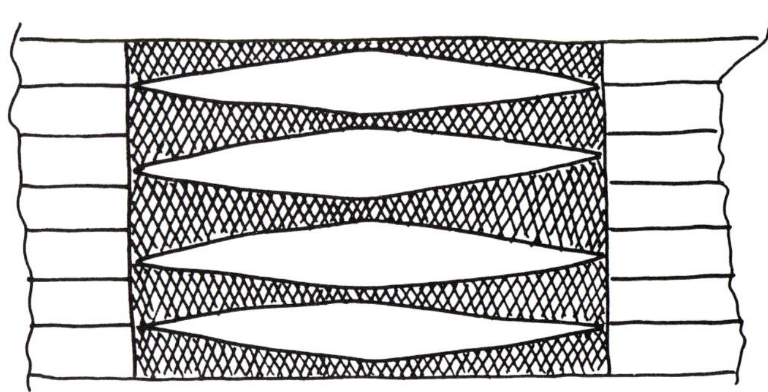

Figure 13. Schematic drawing of a design from an early quilled shirt, ca. 1860.
Peabody Museum, Harvard University.

have red quillwork. A number of hair locks at each elbow have white quillwork, contrasting with the predominate red quillwork on the majority of the sleeve hair locks.

The shirt is further decorated with thirteen black and white golden eagle tail feathers spaced along and fixed in with the quilled hair locks. The feathers have been prepared as for a war bonnet, with the basal end cut into a loop and wrapped with red trade cloth. Seven feathers on the left side of the shirt have been dyed red; the six on the right side of the shirt are in an undyed, natural state. The quilled hair locks and feather decoration are original to the shirt and predate the attachment of the present quilled strips.

The shirt has no helpful collection history or attribution to indicate date of manufacture or tribal origin. Documented history is totally lacking. But because of internal evidence, however, we can postulate a fairly reliable date of ca. 1870 and suggest a Western Sioux or Lakota origin for this garment. The cut and construction, painting style and colors, quillwork technique and patterns and colors, the profusion of quilled hair locks, and even the feather decorations are typical for Sioux shirts of this period. Stylistically, it is a classic example. Among the Lakota, it is the type that was the prerogative of the Wicasas, or the Four Shirt Wearers. The last true Shirt Wearers among the Oglala were American Horse, Crazy Horse, Man Afraid Of His Horse, and Sword. According to Wissler,

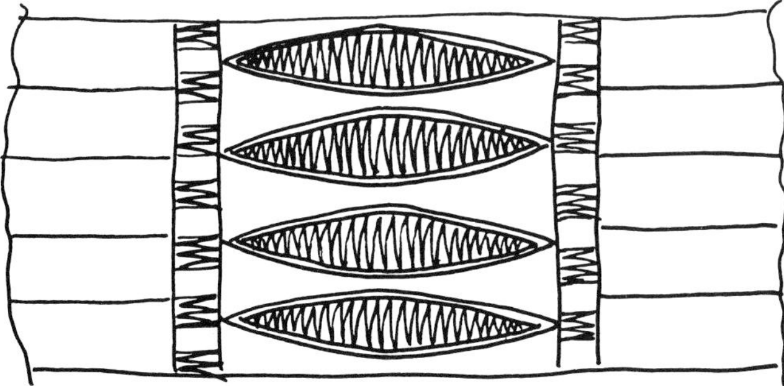

Figure 14. Schematic drawing of a design from an early quilled shirt, ca. 1865. Collected by Thomas Twiss, Indian agent at Ft. Laramie.
Museum of the American Indian, Heye Foundation.

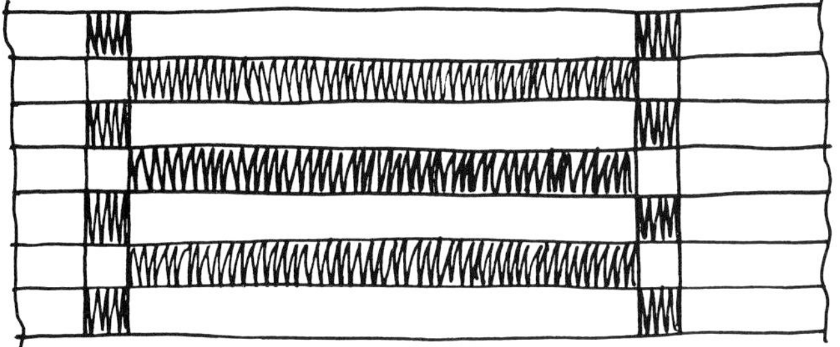

Figure 15. Schematic drawing of the design on the Derby quilled shirt, ca. 1870.

"The four leading men referred to above are the four grand councilors of the Oglala. When chosen by their fellow han skaska members they were formally invested with a shirt similar to the modern scalp shirt. Though in recent times this garment was worn by anyone, it was originally the exclusive regalia of these four men. We are told that the true scalp shirt was made of mountain sheepskin. Two full skins were used. The dew claws were not removed, the skin from the fore legs forming the sleeves, that from the hind legs hung down at the sides. Across the shoulders and down the sleeves were quill-worked bands. Two shirts were painted blue on the upper half and yellow on the lower; the other two had red and yellow halves respectively. The most distinguishing feature, however, was the hair-lock fringe on the sleeve. In theory, at least, a lock of hair was added for each recognized deed in war: as, coup, capturing a horse, taking prisoners, getting wounds, saving the life of a friend, etc., but eventually the fringed shirt became simply the conventional regalia of the four grand councilors and finally a style of dress for anyone."

Amos Bad Heart Bull, in *A Pictographic History of the Oglala Sioux,* shows this type of fringed war shirt as being society regalia for the Brave Hearts, the Smooth Lance Owners, and the Badgers. Through time, shirts have become less emblematic of rank, office, or society affiliation but even today "war shirts" are only worn by important, well-respected Lakota men.

The layout of the patterns on the quilled strips and the designs themselves can be placed in the chronological development scheme of Sioux shirt decoration. The Derby shirt has two design elements on each sleeve and two design elements on the front and back of each shoulder strip. Sioux quilled shirts from an earlier period show a different design placement and also simpler designs. The step-by-step development of pattern can be seen in Figures 12 to 15. In the earlier figure, the patterns are laid in separately and the background lanes are quilled around them. The elongated designs appear to float against the background. In the next step, the elongated designs, sometimes referred to as the "red finger" motif, are still laid in separately but are enclosed within a block, tying the figures to each other and unifying these separate units into a single design element. Figure 14 shows a further elaboration of this same idea.

The Derby shirt shows the next development of this design on quilled Sioux shirts. The "red fingers" are no longer laid in separately and the sides are no longer curved. The "red fingers" become red bars and are worked into the normal lane progression of this type of quillwork. (Figure 15)

The "red finger" pattern worked in quills, as shown on the Twiss shirt, is maintained by the Sioux in their beadwork tradition, as illustrated by the famous Red Cloud shirt and other similar Sioux shirts. And, of course, the bar and block design of the Derby shirt is duplicated in contemporary and later beaded Sioux shirts.

The Derby shirt is remarkable for its adherence to tribal characteristics and for its pristine condition.

The Archetypal Columbia River Plateau Contour Beaded Bag

John M. Gogol

THE INTRODUCTION OF BEADWORK ON THE PLATEAU

The explorers Meriwether Lewis and William Clark were the first white men to traverse the Plateau area of eastern Washington, Idaho, Oregon and Montana. They wrote about what they saw on their travels up and down the Columbia River and its tributaries during their 1805-6 travels. They discovered that the trade in European glass beads had already reached the native Sahaptin Salishan and Chinookan peoples of the area from various sources, and that those beads were among the most treasured of tradegoods.

In the various entries they wrote in their *Journals,* we reexperience the amazement they felt when they saw what an important role trade-beads played in the life of Plateau people. On October 1, 1805, for example, Captain Clark writes about their first experience in trading with the Nez Perce as they entered their territories: ". . . laid out a Small assortment of such articles as those Indians were fond of to trade with them for Some provisions (they are remarkably fond of Beeds)." By November 1, 1805 the Lewis and Clark exploration party was passing through the Cascades of the Columbia River Gorge, on which date Clark enters in his journal the following comments on the local Indian trade economy: ". . . the articles which they appear to trade mostly i.e. Pounded fish, Beargrass, and roots; cannot be an object of commerce with furin merchants. however they git in return for those articles Blue and white *beeds*, copper Kettles, brass arm bands, some scarlet and blue robes and a fiew articles of old clothes,—they prefer beeds to any thing, and will part with the last mouthfull or articles of clothing they ave for a fiew of those beeds,—those beeds they trafick with Indians still higher up this river for roabs, Skins, cha-pel-el (biscuitroot) bread, beargrass, &c. who in their turn trafick with those under the rockey mountains for Beargrass, *quarmash* roots & robes &c."

Following hard on the tracks of the Lewis and Clark expedition, enterprising trappers and fur traders moved onto the Plateau. Important to the development of the beadwork tradition on the Plateau were the arrival of Iroquois, Huron, and other eastern and midwestern area Woodland Indians who were brought into the region by the Northwest Company and others. By 1821, when the Hudson Bay Company had incorporated the Northwest Company, Ross Cox noted that the Iroquois made up "nearly a third of the men employed by the Company on the Columbia."

These adventurous Iroquois warriors brought westward with them fine examples of the arts and crafts of their proud tribes, revealed at their best in the finely crafted quilled and beaded clothing, shot pouches, knife sheaths, and other items that accented their pride in dress. The Indians of the Columbia stood in awe of these proud and aggressive eastern brothers who ostentatiously displayed their wealth and power, which obviously stood in stark contrast to the relative poverty in beads and beadworked items among the locals, at a time when beads were worth their weight in gold, and more.

These finely dressed eastern natives were much envied and soon imitated. Since more Iroquois came west without their families, many soon took local women as wives. Because of their wages and access to tradegoods, the Iroquois trappers were considered wealthy by local standards, and they were able to provide their wives with large quantities of beads to decorate their clothing and other gear. Initially these wives certainly imitated the beading patterns on the clothing and other items their husbands had brought with them from the East, or picked up in the Great Lakes area in their travel westward. Eventually, these were modified by local tastes and traditions to produce a beadwork style unique to the Plateau, such as the Derby contour beaded bag pictured here. (Figure 16, Color Plate 12)

PLATEAU BEADED BAGS

The Plateau area of eastern Washington,

northern Oregon, Idaho, and western Montana produced one of the great beadwork traditions of Native American art,only recently discovered by collectors of Indian art outside of the Pacific Northwest, and about which very little has been written up to the present date. Perhaps the greatest examples of Plateau beadwork were made on the mid-Columbia River and Snake River areas among the Sahaptin Nez Perce, Umatilla, Walla Walla, Yakima, Warm Springs, Tenino, Wyam, Wanapam, Palus, and Klickitats. In addition, the Waiilatpuan-speaking Cayuse were noted for their exceptional finely-executed beadwork, and the Chinookan Wasco and Wishram contributed a unique beadwork tradition derived from their particular long heritage living on the banks of the Columbia.

Plains Indian beadwork has been extensively surveyed in the last few years, with many catalogs of special exhibits providing the basis for writing about the main styles of Plains beadwork among the Sioux, Cheyenne, Arapaho, Crow, and Blackfoot. The only area of Plateau beadwork that has been seriously analyzed in writing are those horsegear and warrior items, particularly the Nez Perce, that obviously have been influenced by the trade in horses with the Plains tribes to the east.

The most common beadwork item on the Plateau, however, is the beaded bag, and it is the item about which almost nothing has been written so far. Yet, it is the art form that became unique to the Plateau, both in technique and design. The overwhelming presence of these bags in old photos of Plateau people emphasize not only the large quantity of these that were made, but also their role as personal, family, and tribal prestige items. By the 1860s and 1870s, they had already come to fill the same role as cornhusk bags, as gift-giving and "dress up" items, treasures made for personal and tribal functions, not items made for the tourist trade.

Figure 16. Nez Perce contour beaded bag (pouch) sewn on native tanned buckskin with buckskin fringe; red, lavender, pumpkin, yellow, white, medium and dark blue Venetian glass beads. 35 cm long (including fringe), 15.5 cm wide (at top). The main body of the bag is beaded in typical Plateau sewn appliqué beadwork, while the top flap is done in lazy stitch.

THE 1850s

The 1850s were a critical time in the development of beadwork. Writers analyzing the development of the bandolier bag among the western Great Lakes tribes, such as the Ojibwe and Winnebago, have noted the tremendous growth in the production of these beaded items in the second half of the nineteenth century, and their scarcity before 1850. This is also true on the Plateau, and one of the main reasons for this development was obviously the settlement of the tribes onto reservations—the outgrowth of peace treaties during that decade. Reservations brought large numbers of tribal peoples together into a relatively sedentary existence, where native crafts provided opportunity for activity, maintenance of tribal pride and tradition, and the personal opportunity to excel and produce something of extraordinary value. With the natives settled on reservations, traders moved in to offer trade-goods in quantity, including beads, on a convenient and regularly accessible basis.

This author believes that the typical beaded Plateau bag was a development that branched out of the tradition of the cornhusk bag, that most original and unique Plateau art form. It was after the 1850s that the cornhusk bag made the transition from more utilitarian to more prestige item, which was then complemented by the beaded bag as special "dress-up" and gift-giving object. The relationship to the cornhusk bag tradition explains the large beaded bag tradition that arose on the Plateau and almost not at all on the Plains, except as a few were traded in that direction. In surveying collections of beadwork made among the Blackfeet, Crow, Sioux, and Cheyenne, the Plateau type bag is not to be found. One finds the pipebags, small accessory pouches, belt pouches, and beaded commercially made bags, but no large flat bags. (See for example Audrey Porsche's *Yuto'keca: Transitions, The Burdick Collection* (Sioux beadwork); Walton, Ewers, and Hassrick's *After the Buffalo Were Gone, The Louis Warren Hill, Sr., Collection of Indian Art* (Blackfeet beadwork); and Richard Conn's *A Persistent Vision, Art of the Reservation Days* (Arapaho, Cheyenne, Sioux, Blackfeet, and Crow beadwork).

CONTOUR BEADED FLORAL DESIGN BAGS

The contour beaded bag certainly began as a man's wearing item, in imitation of the uses seen among the intrusive Iroquois and other eastern Woodland men on the Plateau. The stylized floral patterns that form the basis of all early Plateau contour bags also were formed from the influence of these eastern Indians on the Plateau. These floral patterns that became an essential design pattern in Woodland Indian beadwork have been explained as possibly derived from the embroidery traditions taught by French nuns working among the natives of eastern Canada, and possibly also influenced from the Algonquin Indian birch bark basketry tradition. The double curve motif forms the basis of the beadwork traditions among the eastern Woodland Indians, as well as of all early contour bags on the Plateau. This motif is formed by any variation of the symmetrical curving away from a central point. Some theorize that this formal pattern arose from the practice of Algonquin women folding pieces of birch bark, and then biting or otherwise punching patterns into them, which, when unfolded, reveal perfectly symmetrical patterns.

On the Plateau, the floral motif pattern was early simplified into a much bolder design configuration, which became a part of the unique heritage of beadwork on the Columbia River. In early eastern beadwork, as well as in the earliest examples on the Plateau, only the design element was beaded, with the background consisting of the red or blue tradecloth backing.

With the coming of the reservation era during the late 1850s, beads had become much more readily available so that beadworkers could then fill in the background to create fully beaded bags. White and light blue became the overwhelming choice for background colors, making for a strong contrast to the darker tradecloth backgrounds of earlier partially beaded bags.

In the flowing double-curved motif floral patterns, the beads were sewn to the fabric or buckskin in an appliqué stitch. When the beadworker acquired enough beads to fill in the background, it was only natural to apply the background beads following the same curvilinear lines of the main motifs, the result producing the contour effect. Thus, this method of sewing on the background beads may be seen to have been a matter of practicality (though in a later beadwork tradition on the Plateau, beadworkers did sew the background beads in straight line patterns horizontally across the face of the bag).

The curved lines of the background bead patterns, however, may be seen to have been done for another reason, i.e. to protect spiritual values. Curved background lines may be seen to be projections of the items being encircled, part of an art tradition seen in other tribal arts from Africa to North America, as well as in early Christian, Egyptian, and Hindu painting. The surrounding lines project the spirit force, the magnetic force field, of the central figure, just like the halos painted around Christian saints.

Most Native American groups believed that every object, plant, and animal had a spirit, a power, a life-energy force that existed separate from the physical object, exerting a kind of spiritual magnetic force around it. The Huichol Indians of Mexico, for example, picture such contour force fields surrounding the power flowers of the holy peyote plant in their colorful colored yarn and beeswax paintings.

The roots of flowering plants were one of the mainstays of life on the Plateau, and the dependence on roots like camas and bitterroot for survival during the winter months is still celebrated in Plateau tribal root festivals on both the Warm Springs and Yakima reservations, as well as among the Nez Perce. These roots were sacred foods to which songs were sung before gathering and preparation, and the flowering manifestations of the blue camas and pink bitterroot were a magical guide to the world beneath the ground that produced food that was both staple and sacrament. Thus it is not surprising that the contour bag—initially a foreign artform, derived from the floral patterns of eastern Indian beadwork—flourished, transformed into a dynamic and colorful celebration of the spiritual life of native plants.

Early contour bags of the 1850s through the 1870s are inevitably symmetrical, following the strictures of the double curve motif, but toward the end of the century, the floral patterns change, become more naturalistic and depart from the rules of symmetry. At first the sacred salmon, elk, and deer are introduced, followed later by horses, birds, and butterflies. In the 1920s, the types of beads used have changed dramatically as well as the variations in bead application styles, and the tradition has moved away from the magical/sacred toward folk art.

The fully contoured beaded Plateau bag of the 1850s through the 1870s is a true classic piece of Native American art, unique from what came before and after, and as much a treasure as the classic Navajo wearing blanket or the Dat-So-La-Lee Washoe basket—all items produced within a certain time period, and the best of their kind.

THE ARCHETYPAL PLATEAU CONTOUR BAG

When Charles Derby asked me to identify this beaded bag and to decide whether it belonged to the Plateau, as various beadwork collectors who had seen it had placed its origin in various parts of the country, I replied that it was not only a Plateau bag, but an archetypal Plateau contour beaded bag. So, what are the elements that place the origins of this bag on the Plateau, and make it an archetype from the area and era?

The structural nature of the archetypal fully contoured beaded Plateau bag consists of a three-part division of the floral design element both horizontally and vertically. The stem of the leafed floral plant that forms the main design runs exactly down the center of the bag. Attached symmetrically to each side of that stem are a combination of three leaves or flowers, in almost any combination, with a central floral motif that usually tops the stem, but sometimes is a central motif. (See *American Indian Basketry and Other Native Arts* No. 18, pg. 7.) The leaf and flower patterns are usually heavily outlined, sometimes double outlined, with the outermost line in a color darker than the background or central color of the flower/leaf. In addition the flower/leaf motifs, which are sometimes so stylized that it is hard to distinguish which is flower and which is leaf, are arranged in combinations of three horizontally. Occasionally there is an extra element at the bottom, top, or in the corners, but the three-part division both horizontally and vertically is dominant and obvious.

The earliest contour bags are rounded at the bottom, as in the Derby bag. This bag has three elements above the base in the main column, and is flanked by three design elements on each side, with the base element repeated again in each side element to again form three matching elements. The number three is, of course, almost a universal magical/spiritual number, and has religious significance in many cultures. The design in the

Derby bag so strongly departs from naturalistic portrayal of the floral design that the uninitiated might not even recognize the floral and leaf patterns in the design, and we are all left wondering at the fantastic blue outlined white patterns at the top of the side columns. What might be seen as fingers of a hand might be the petals of the blue camas (edible camas) and white camas (death camas). In other bags there are variations on this tripartite division, sometimes with the addition of some other central motif, but all other elements are usually added in some combination of three, with the maintenance of the symmetrical curvilinear pattern.

The red background beads in the Derby bag were sewn on after the main design elements were applied, and they appear as accenting curvilinear halos, or waves, emanating from the surface outlines of the power-filled flower/leaf motifs.

The Derby bag is a Nez Perce man's personal effects bag and possibly at one time was attached to a bandolier strap. The fringe and the lazy stitch beaded flap are not typical for the majority of Plateau contour beaded bags, but place it in the category of those early bags made for men under the influence of Plains decorating techniques, while the main body of the bag remains classic Plateau art.

Firebags of the Fur Trade

Ted J. Brasser

The Derby Collection includes two exquisite examples of perhaps the most enigmatic types of pouches in North American Indian collections. I refer here to artifacts usually referred to as octopus bags and panel bags.

Octopus bags are often made of dark blue, black, or red broadcloth, about 40 to 50 cm. long and 25 to 35 cm. wide. The upper edge of this flat bag is either curved as a whole or rounded at the corners, and is often somewhat narrower at the top than at the lower part of the bag. Many of these bags have a round worsted closing cord, held at the upper front by two brass buttons and reeved through two corresponding holes in the back of the pouch. Extending downward from the bottom are four pairs of tabs with indented ends, finished with bead-strung fringes that terminate in tassles of red wool yarn. Due to these tentacles, the bag's modern name refers to the octopus, though in earlier times they were called fire bags, as they were used to hold the pipe, tobacco, and ingredients to make fire. One or both sides of the bag is decorated with floral motifs in silk embroidery or with spot-stitched beadwork in at least four—but often more—different colors. When both sides of the pouch are decorated, these two patterns are different from each other. The edges of the pouch and tabs are bound with colored silk ribbon, outlined with white beads. The bag and the tabs are frequently lined with cotton fabric, and all sewing and beading of these bags is usually done with cotton thread.

The panel bags were also made of dark blue or red trade cloth, in the same range of sizes as the octopus bag. The upper edge of this flat bag may be curved but the rest of the bag has a rectangular shape. The panel of loom-woven beadwork that is attached along the bottom edge of the bag is also rectangular. The sides and lower rim of this panel are decorated with fringes terminating in red yarn tassels. Bars of contrasting colors were often created by means of the beads strung on these fringes.

Some of these panel bags have a drawstring in the upper part, similar to the arrangement on octopus bags. The decoration with floral motifs in silk embroidery or beads is also similar, though the earlier examples tend to be either plain or decorated with ribbon appliqué. Contrasting with the variety of floral patterns is the limited range of rigidly geometric motifs in the loom-woven panels. Some of these bags are lined with cotton fabric, and cotton thread was used in the sewing and beading of most panel bags.

Figure 17. Octopus bag, Red River Metis type, ca. 1890. (See cover for other side of bag)

There is something enigmatic about these two bag types due to the fact that large numbers of them can be found, particularly in Canadian collections, but few of these pouches are associated with documentation concerning their origin and/or age. These two characteristics—that is, their large numbers versus their poor documentation—are the strength and the weakness in the study of these pouches. This situation is reminiscent of the potsherds and arrow heads studied by the archaeologist, suggesting a typological classification as the most obvious strategy in the study of these bags. Differences in shape and fringes have indeed made it possible to distinguish a number of sub-types, but the amazing variety in their decoration strongly suggests a greater difference in time and space that has so far defied its definition.

Assuming that the decorative patterns on these bags represent a tribal or regional art style, a comparative survey was made of beadwork that originated from the northern Plains and the neighboring Sub-arctic. Despite similarities found in certain regions, however, the decorative patterns on panel bags and octopus bags turned out to be rather unique, having more in common with each other than with the beadwork on other items. This suggests that these bags originated from a region or were produced by people of which we know very little.

Whereas most of these bags were made of and decorated with materials imported by the fur traders, it is significant that they have their prototypes in the early historic art of the Great Lakes Indians. Rectangular skin bags, provided at the bottom with either tabs and fringes, or with a panel of netted quillwrapped fringes, were made by these Indians as early as 1720 and as late as the 1780s. They were decorated with painted geometric designs, different from each other on both sides of the bag. A few bags of this type were collected west of the Great Lakes as late as the 1820s, and the use of tabs and woven panels at the bottom of pipe bags survived among the Western Sioux and Cheyenne Indians in the late nineteenth century. It is evident that the octopus bags and panel bags to be discussed here were more recent interpretations of the ancient pouch types of the Great Lakes Indians.

With respect to octopus bags, the following notes are based on a corpus of 139 examples, including thirty bags of which location and period of acquisition are known. These data indicate that the first octopus bags were acquired in southern Manitoba in the 1840s, but within the next ten years a distinct type was also made by the Cree of northern Manitoba. In the same period, a third type became popular along the Missouri River, decorated with beadwork patterns reminiscent of the curvilinear style adopted by the Yankton and Yanktonai Sioux. Nevertheless, these three early types of octopus bags had still much in common, suggesting intimate contacts with the lower Red River in southern Manitoba. These three centers continued to produce octopus bags for several decades, but after 1860 other sub-types appeared in more and more northwestern regions. Octopus bags decorated with very elaborate floral patterns became popular in northern Saskatchewan and northern Alberta, followed by somewhat simplified versions in the interior of British Columbia. These northwestern octopus bags, in particular, present an incredible variety in their decoration. Of the thirty documented octopus bags, at least seventeen were acquired at trading posts or from people associated with the fur trade.

By 1870, the fashion had reached the Tlingit Indians on the Northwest coast, giving rise to the development of a unique style of semi-floral beadwork among these people. Octopus bags of the Missouri River type had now also reached the lower Columbia River in Oregon. After 1920, however, the popularity of octopus bags rapidly declined, although their manufacture and use survived in northwestern Ontario as late as the 1980s.

The octopus bag in the Derby Collection is made of black trade cloth, 54 cm. long including the fringe, 22.5 cm. wide, and lined with white cotton. Its rectangular shape, straight upper rim with rounded corners, and the space left between the tabs are typical features of the style that originated in the Red River region of Manitoba in the 1840s. This shape was also maintained for top quality bags made in northern Alberta after 1860. The rather wide spaces between the tabs of this bag are filled with long fringes, which is a feature that can be traced back to the ancient skin pouches made in the Great Lakes region. Such long fringes between the tabs are found on the octopus bags from Manitoba up to the 1850s, and they survived on some bags from northern

Alberta. Definitely old-fashioned, too, is the use of large oval white beads on the fringes of the tabs; such beads have been noticed only on early octopus bags from Manitoba.

The floral patterns on both sides of the Derby bag are of a rigidly bilaterally symmetric type, in which an unnatural variety of leaves, buds, flowers, and spirals are evenly distributed on both sides of a thin, straight, central stem. The composition is reminiscent of the style represented by the early Red River bags, but the floral elements are of a more northwestern type. On bags of the latter type—those from northern Alberta and Great Slave Lake—such floral elements were combined by thick hairy stems in dense, complex, and asymmetrical compositions. Interesting are the two twirling rosettes on one side of the Derby bag; they are of a type that was most popular among the Sekani Indians of northeastern British Columbia.

The octopus bag in the Derby Collection presents in its shape and decorative elements a combination of the early Manitoba type and more recent features that are characteristic for bags from northwestern Alberta and the adjacent part of the Northwest Territories. In addition, there are indications of contact with the native people of northeastern British Columbia. In this combination, the retention of early Manitoba elements suggests a conservative attitude of the producer—a woman acquainted with the Red River art style of the 1850s. However, she was no longer living there; she may have resided at, say, Fort Nelson in the 1890s, exposed to the more recent art developments in northwestern Alberta and adjacent British Columbia. The result of these diverse influences is an octopus bag that in its decorations is quite distinct from the embroidery of the regional Slave and Sekani Indians. Many top-quality octopus bags present this difference with regional native art, suggesting that their producers were distinct from the local native people. Also striking is that the historic spread of these octopus bags coincides with the major routes and centers of the fur trade. Thus it seems that the producers of these octopus bags were people who excelled in making floral beadwork, but were more intimately associated with the trading posts than with the regional Indian communities. These considerations direct the spotlight of our search to the Red River Metis and their descendants, often referred to as the "Flower Beadwork People" by the Indians.

Figure 18. Panel bag, Kaska type?, ca. 1860. (See color plate 11 for other side of bag)

After the American War of Independence, developments in the Great Lakes region forced the local fur traders to move to more western frontiers. With them went many of the Ojibwa or Saulteaux Indians, as well as a considerable part of the halfbreed, or Metis, population. In contrast to the Indians who visited the trading posts only for short periods, these "French Metis" had always made great efforts to let their children profit from the local mission schools. There they became acquainted with embroidery in a floral style, and this art form became a hallmark of Metis culture in the nineteenth century.

When the fur trade moved west, Metis settlements were established at several places along the Missouri River, the upper Mississippi and northward along the lower Red River. Most of these Metis remained employed by trade companies, but particularly in the upper Mississippi region, quite a number of them intermarried with the local Sioux Indians and became free traders.

Afraid of losing its western clientele, the Hudson's Bay Company also established trading posts on the Red River and westward along the Saskatchewan in the 1770's. This company had long since depended upon Cree Indians and Cree-Metis in its contacts with more remote native people. In 1821, the intense rivalry between the Northwest Company and the Hudson's Bay Company came to an end when they united.

As a result, a large part of their Metis employees were laid off, forcing them to make their livelihood as buffalo hunters and independent traders. Part of their merchandise included horse bridles, saddles, skin coats, moccasins, and various pouches, all of them elaborately decorated by their wives.

Many of these Metis made their residence at Pembina and more northern locations along the Red River, a large part found employment in the American fur trade along the Missouri River, and Metis settlements were established near Fort Edmonton and other locations in the northwest. A number of Metis joined the Yanktonai Sioux, who adopted them as a separate band in their tribe. The distribution of Metis family names from St. Louis in the south to the Saskatchewan in the north reflected the mobility and far-ranging social ties that remained a distinctive aspect of Metis society during the fur trade era. Promoted by the sheer size of this population, these and other factors fostered the emergence of an ethnic awareness and a cultural identity that became visible in the arts and crafts of these Metis. This development was most evident on the Red River. Nevertheless, these Metis never abandoned their ancestral ties with the Saulteaux and Cree Indians.

Not surprisingly, Metis work is often difficult to distinguish from that of their native relatives. Due to the very nature of Metis society, moreover, the Metis art style influenced the changing fashions of practically every tribal group on the northern Plains and in the Canadian northwest. Yet, many of the bags in early ethnographic collections from western Canada show in their decoration the fusion of diverse art styles that became characteristic for the Red River Metis and their descendants. The octopus bag in the Derby Collection is a fine example of their work.

It was decided to discuss Charles Derby's octopus bag and his panel bag in the same essay, because the history and development of these two bag types seems to coincide to a large degree.

Rectangular skin bags, decorated with painted designs and a panel of netted quill-wrapped fringes at the bottom, were used by Great Lakes Indians during the eighteenth century. Between 1780 and 1820, similar bags originated from Minnesota and the Red River. Several of these later bags were decorated in quillwork with stylized and delicate floral patterns that are unknown from earlier collections. These quill-worked panel bags were the ancestors of the bag being discussed here. The following notes are based on the study of seventy similar bags, twenty of which have a documentation concerning their origin and age.

By 1830, if not somewhat earlier, a standard type of panel bag evolved on the Red River. In the manufacture of this bag, skin and quillwork rapidly gave way to imported trade cloth and beads. Although there was occasionally some ribbon work on these panel bags, their major decoration consisted of the loom-woven beadwork panel at the bottom, surrounded by bead-strung fringes and red yarn tassels. Woven in the panel was a geometric pattern of which close equivalents were popular in loom-woven quillwork from the region. This quillwork is usually attributed to the Manitoba Cree, but it also decorated much of the horse gear traded by the Red River Metis. These beadworked panel bags are visible in at least two portraits made of Red River Metis in the 1850s (Brasser, in Peterson and Brown, 1985).

By that time, the fashion appears to have already reached as far west as the interior of British Columbia and the lower Columbia River, although there is hardly any evidence of panel bags on the northwestern Plains. Their occurrence west of the Rocky Mountains may be related to the emigration of Red River people to the Columbia River in 1841 and in 1854. Information on the art of the native people in the interior of British Columbia and Washington in the nineteenth century is rather scarce and restricted to "traditional" expressions such as basketry. Further research in photo archives and museum collections may provide more details on the distribution and topology of both octopus and panel bags in that region.

After 1870 panel bags became popular among the Swampy Cree from northern Manitoba eastward to the James Bay region, initiating the development of two distinct sub-types. By 1880, panel bags were also made by the Inland Tlingit on the upper Yukon River.

The panel bag in the Derby Collection is made of black cloth, 19.5 cm. long and 17 cm. wide. The panel of woven beadwork and fringe at the bottom adds 14.5 cm. to its length. The inside of the bag is lined with cotton print. It has its rectangular shape in common with early panel bags from the Red River, as well as with those made in the interior of British Columbia. The style of its decoration is different from that of the early Red River bags and points to a late-nineteenth century origin in a more northwestern region. Unusual—if not unique—is the use of white porcupine quills as the bindings that hold the yarn tassels together.

The use of 'hairy' flower and leaf patterns on one side of the bag is reminiscent of Metis work on the upper Mackenzie River in the 1880s, and so is the white zig-zag pattern that borders the other side of the bag. No such panel bags are known from that region, however, and there are a number of elements that point to a more western and earlier origin. The thistles and open leaf forms on one side of the bag, and the stars in the most unusual pattern of the woven panel, occur on bags that appear to have been made in northern British Columbia in the late 1860s. My guess is that this panel bag was made by Kaska Indians, or by Metis in Kaska territory, about 1870.

The study of Red River Metis art history is still in an early stage and raises more questions than can be answered at present. Unless we find more documented material, many of these octopus bags and panel bags will forever remain an enigma in the ethnographic collections. Related and equally urgent is the need for more information on the art of the western Wood Cree, the Beaver, and their western neighbors.

However fragmentary our knowledge may be at present, sufficient evidence indicates that the Red River Metis and their descendants played an important role in the development of a flamboyant art style among the native people in the Canadian northwest. This development appears to have run its course before the arrival of anthropologists in the region, as few of them made any reference to it in their reports.

Apache Dress in the Derby Collection

Benson L. Lanford

In his introduction to *The Indians of Texas in 1830,* John C. Ewers informs us that in 1826, at about twenty years of age, Jean Louis Berlandier left France for Mexico to serve as biologist for an official exploring expedition into Texas, Mexico's then northernmost province. Berlandier collected remarkably important materials during this commission and during the succeeding two decades while he lived in Matamoros (across the Rio Grande from present-day Brownsville, Texas). His assemblage of regional Native American material culture is now in the collections of the Smithsonian Institution, and boasts of one of the most important nineteenth-century Southern Plains garments to survive to the present.

Object number USNM 1480 is a painted and fringed sleeveless poncho worn separately as a dress top, illustrated in the above work by Jean Louis Berlandier. All but one object in the Berlandier Collection are attributed to the Comanche. The cape in the Berlandier Collection closely resembles the cape of a beautiful two-piece dress in the Derby Collection.

"Berlandier was not content with a written description of the Indians of Texas. He complemented his manuscript with a unique graphic record prepared under his supervision. It consists of 18 watercolors picturing men and women of 16 tribes. All of these paintings bear the signature of a little-known artist, Lino Sanchez y Tapia. A majority of them, however, are clearly designated after originals by a Lieutenant Jose Maria Sanchez y Tapia, the artist-cartographer of the expedition, or after Berlandier himself. That both of these men possessed considerable artistic talent is proved by examples of their original drawings preserved in the archives of the Western Americana Collection at Yale and of the Gray Herbarium Library at Harvard. These watercolors of Indians are not true scenes, but rather representations of old costume in the tradition of the European fashion plate. They are not intended as portraits of particular Indians, and the settings are conventionalized. . . ."[1] These drawings give us some of the precious few early nineteenth-century images of Southern Plains Indians and their garments.

In addition to numerous males, six women illustrated in as many watercolors in this series give graphic clues to female clothing in vogue in the region at that time. The tribes recorded are the Tonkawa, Tawakoni, Karankawa, Cocos, Comanche, and Lipan Apache. The Tonkawa woman is bare-breasted, but wears a simple skirt, probably of tanned animal hide. Her skirt bears no decoration; however, points of skin project below the lower margin at the sides. These may be seen in five of the watercolors as well as on the Derby skirt.

In another painting, a Comanche woman wears a two-piece skin garment. The plain, short-sleeved top is undecorated except for a simple self-fringe at the bottom. A projection of skin extends below the margin at each side of the skirt. She wears moccasins that appear to have a seam from the toe to instep and short, turned-up cuffs over the ankles. These differ from the high-top moccasins associated with Wichita, Comanche, Kiowa, Apache, Cheyenne, and Arapaho women later in the century. The painting of the Tawakoni woman clearly illustrates high-top moccasins extending to mid-calf.

Perhaps the watercolor most significant to this paper depicts an Apache woman wearing a two-piece skin garment, red-brown overall. The neck and bottom of the large, flaring poncho-cape are fringed, the skirt is fringed along the bottom, and a row of fringe is added at lower mid-point. She also wears undecorated slipper-like moccasins. (It is of interest to note that low-cut moccasins are worn by the Cocos woman as well as the Apache and Comanche women. The low-cut moccasin type will be expounded upon in discussing the Derby pair.) These renderings establish the fact that two-piece garments and ankle-high moccasins were used by at least three tribes in Texas during the early nineteenth century. Two-piece dresses are still worn by numbers of Southern Plains women, although in reservation times the one-piece dress seems to have been more prevalent. The former is considerably more comfortable in that hot region, enjoys a resurgence of fashion from time to time, and is even preferred in some tribes.

Careful tanning of skins on the Southern Plains was a highly regarded art. Beadwork decoration of skin clothing was minimal and porcupine quillwork was virtually unknown. However, elaborate fringing—in addition to painting with gathered and traded commercial powdered pigments in various shades of red, yellow, blue, and green—served to elaborate tailored garments such as shirts, leggings, dresses, and moccasins. Deerskins were used predominantly to construct these articles; however, antelope were extensively hunted and their skins were undoubtedly used as well. Precise care was taken in all tanning steps to produce unblemished, uniform, and soft—but tough—results. Incidental holes were covered by a variety of methods, which yielded barely noticeable patches. "Buckskin" is a popular term used to refer to tanned animal skins regardless of the sex or species of a given animal. However, buffalo and cow hides are usually recognizable and therefore the term "buckskin" is not applicable. On the Northern Plains, where garments with a great deal of quill and beadwork were produced, such care was not always given to the tanning process. On the Southern Plains, however, prime buckskin was always at a premium.

Various Apache groups were the principal Central Plains inhabitants in proto-historic and historic times. Such terms as *Lipan, Cantsi, Natage, Quirache, Carlana, Sierra Blanca, Faragon, Gataka, Paloma, Paducah, Llanero,* and *Mescalero* punctuate recorded historic accounts of these peoples and the region. Undoubtedly, these Apaches influenced others who arrived later, sharing material culture objects in general and clothing patterns in particular. Among these was the woman's two-piece skin dress, which is still being worn at present, especially among the major Southern Plains tribes.

The Derby dress and moccasins are remarkably beautiful in the primitive sense, and embody all of the qualities desirable in this art form:

Figure 19. Back of dress (See color plate 14 for front)

superb hide tanning, handsome painting, exquisite buckskin cutting and assemblage, minimal but precise beadwork, a profusion of metal cones, and overall artfulness and design. They are at once recognizable as the work of a true master of her craft, resulting from many industrious years. On the surface, this remarkable ensemble appears to be simple, but an in-depth description will reveal its complexity.

YOKE

A single, large, medium-smoked deerskin turned hair side out forms the dress top or yoke. The most noteworthy feature of this half of the garment is the large, uncolored Maltese Cross-like design contrasted against a dark, yellow-orange ochre background. The design essentially covers the entire yoke, front and back identical. This configuration is remarkably similar to that painted on the Berlandier yoke. It, however, is rendered in the opposite manner—the motif painted, the background plain. The outline of the unpainted motif on the Derby yoke is highlighted with a band of lazystitch beadwork using only three beads per stitch—white, pony trader blue, and white, successively. The blue is a translucent medium blue.

The undecorated neck opening is a slit cut across the width of the hide so that its length extends tail end to the back and head end to the front, when worn over the shoulders. The center point of the back lower margin is even with that of the front. When the yoke is spread flat this border is seen to be cut straight, but because the rear of a hide is wider, the outer edges hang longer. The neck portion of the skin forms a crescent at the lower front. Thirteen stepped scallops are cut into this margin. A short, doubled fringe is passed through itself as it skewers the corner of each step. About half of the contiguous skin of each leg is present, the tips cut square, hair intact. These form a pendant at the four corners of the yoke.

A wide, doubled strip of unpainted hide is sewn with sinew along the two outer edges of the yoke. This addition is cut into long fringes to within ¾″ of the yoke proper, furnishing a plain border to the painted area and covering the wearer's arms in a sleeve-like manner. Each fringe is slightly twisted. Along the entire back bottom margin and the two unscalloped areas of the front bottom margin, a relatively narrow strip of painted hide has been doubled, sewn, and fringed. These fringes have been wetted, pulled to obtain maximum length, and slightly twisted. Meticulously cut fringes typify Southern Plains and Apache garments as much as do carefully tanned hides. That fringing is an important aspect of craftwork is exemplified by this dress. Long doubled fringes are suspended across the midpoint, painted to conform to the yoke proper. One individual, broken fringe has been tied back together to maintain integrity. In addition, one black pony bead has been threaded onto one of these long fringes, and the remains of a small tab of deerskin with the hair is affixed to another. It is possible that these were emblematic of personal medicine.

Additional ornamentation on the yoke includes four small brass hawk bells attached at intervals to the long fringes. Also from near each end of the neck opening, four relatively large metal disks are suspended at the ends of doubled, red-ochred thongs that terminate in a small tassle of buckskin fringes. One disk is a silver hair plate with a central bar, 2¾″ in diameter.[2] Serrations are filed around its outer edge. Two other 3″ disks are doubly pierced with a small single hole on opposite margins. The fourth measures 3½″ and has but one piercing at one margin.

A "turkey beard" is a clump of black hairlike feathers that protrudes from the breast of male wild turkeys. At the midpoint of the yoke front, a section of cropped beard held together by what appears to be a section of skin and adhering cartilage is attached to a thong. The base of this has been pierced as for suspension, and is wrapped with red stroud cloth, white seed beads, and a buckskin thong. Turkey beard has been seen on other historic Apache dress tops. Its presence is most likely symbolic. Additional research may explain this custom. Elbys Hugar, a Chiricahua informant who lives on the Mescalero Reservation in south-central New Mexico, stated that her people attach turkey beard to the top of a baby's cradleboard.

The yoke has no true sleeves, nor is it sewn or laced together under the arms. The entire deerskin making up the garment creates a full, draped effect. It is worn like a poncho, just covering the skirt top belted at the waist.

Perhaps the most engaging, charming and meaningful, though problematic, feature of the yoke is a small, elongated animal figure painted in red ochre inside the bottom back near the edge, close to the leg skin extension (see figure 20). It is approximately 1½″ long, has four legs and a downward-pointing tail. The feet are not represented. An earlike point rises from the head. The face is pointed. It is possible to conjecture at

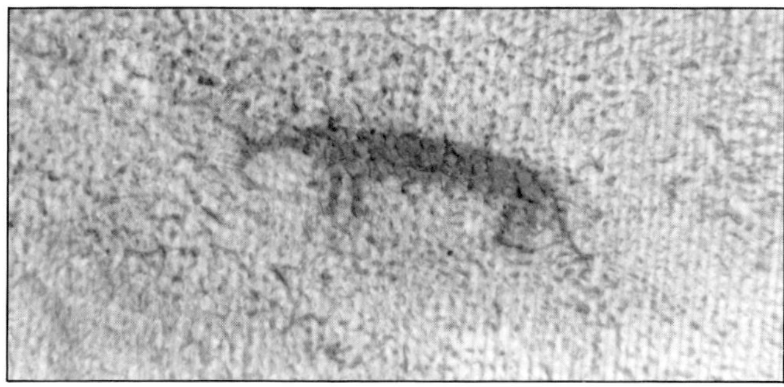

Figure 20. Animal figure painted inside of yoke.

length about this animal. Native Americans did not normally sign or mark objects to indicate the maker or personal ownership, but it is possible that this animal refers to the owner's name, family or band affiliation. It may be a personal totem, charm or protective device, or could have represented a benevolent creature to petition for the bestowal of favors. It is an uncommon and certainly meaningful addition to this garment. To speculate about the animal's exact species would be to court dubiety. Often Native American depiction of particular animals is stylized and may not be automatically recognizable.

SKIRT

The two skins comprising the skirt are sewn together with sinew, flesh side turned out. The skirt therefore has a nappier surface than the yoke. Even some historic Southern Plains dresses that have the yoke and skirt joined exhibit this arrangement—either the yoke or the skirt hair side out, and vice versa. The two seams that close the sides taper from the outer edge at the top to a point recessed 1½″ at the bottom. This provides a double, fringed flap on each side. The bottom of the skirt is folded back onto itself and cut into points. These are laced to the skirt proper by knotted thongs clipped short after tying.

The skirt front and back are similarly painted with areas of yellow, red, and red-orange ochre. Overall, the back is plainer. The long extensions formed by deer leg skin are painted vertically, half and half, in two colors. A 5″-wide band of hide sewn below the skirt top forms a "tunic" across the front. A band of black and white lazy-stitch beadwork covers the stitching. The upper third is painted dark yellow, and the remainder red. The bottom margin of this band is cut into points, which are in turn skewered with short pendant thongs through the tips. A row of long thongs and a second row of short thongs with metal cones are threaded through the tunic. Metal cones are spangled at various points on the skirt, particularly in a vertical row on the bottom side pendants. A horizontal line of spot-stitched white seed beads demarcates the two distinctly painted halves. A number of scars left from fly larvae are present in the upper portion of the back skirt panel. These resisted the powdered pigment used to color the hides. A number of small holes in the hides were not patched. It is not unusual to find unpatched holes in skin clothing.

Accessories to the dress are a paint pouch and awl case. These are loosely tied to long fringes of the skirt front. The former is of tanned skin and measures 6″ by 2½″. It is covered with lazystitch beadwork in dark clear red and white pony beads. Metal cones are suspended from the rounded flap and straight bottom. Two lanes of pony beads in a checked pattern decorate the back, and bead-strung thongs hang from the bottom corners. The sides are sewn with sinew; each stitch carries a white pony bead. This type of bag closely resembles the "strike-a-light" pouches common to the entire Plains region, but contains powdered Chinese vermillion pigment.

The awl case measures 9½″ long and has pony beads only on the thong streamers. The case proper is fully worked with faceted brass, dark clear red, and pony-trader blue seed beads. Along with white, the latter two colors were favorite choices of the Kiowa and Comanche in the past century, with dark, clear red frequently used as background. The combination of pony beads and seed beads in Plains art indicates manufacture during the 1850s or 1860s, but it is difficult to ascertain the tribal origin of much pony beadwork for lack of distinguishing tribal characteristics. However, these two objects are not typical of Apache art. There is no way to determine if they are original to the ensemble; indeed they could have been added at any time. Therefore, the paint pouch and awl case are not viable clues to the tribal origin or manufacture date of the dress and moccasins.

DISCUSSION

The Southern Plains two-piece dress is undoubtedly ancient. It is a logical result of using large animal skins for clothing: two for the skirt and one for the yoke, "waist" or "top." Two-piece dresses are reported from the Kiowa, Comanche, and various Apache groups, including the Kiowa-Apache. The Southern Arapaho and Cheyenne seem to have traditionally employed only the one-piece dress; however, the data are confusing. Beginning at least with the reservation period and continuing to the present, both styles of garment appear to have been used by the first two groups mentioned above. It seems that the traditional two-piece ensemble has remained *de rigueur* among the various Apache groups. The two-piece arrangement of skirt and yoke was evidently joined by some groups at some point in history to form a one-piece article of apparel. Yet, others probably never used a two-piece combination. Still, some adopted a one-piece and used it along with the two-piece, or even dropped the two-piece for a period of time, only to revive its use later.

Elbys Hugar was kind enough to study photographs of the Derby dress, as well as photographs, drawings, and slides of other historic Apache material culture examples. She freely gave her opinions of the images, stating that the Derby dress was definitely Apache but not Chiricahua, Lipan or Mescalero—tribal bands local to the Mescalero Reservation. Mrs. Hugar explained that a two-piece dress of this type can be called a "puberty dress" and is made by a female relative of a young woman for her "Na-i-es" or "coming out" ceremony, usually a four-day ritual attended by relatives and friends in recognition of the girl attaining womanhood. The "Ganhe" ("Ganni" or "Gan"),[1] or "Mountain Spirits," attend and dance as part of the observance and blessing. The puberty dress is highly prized and may be kept as a family heirloom, handed down for generations. During her life, a woman may wear the dress at any special occasion she chooses. Hence, they are seen in photographs from any era. Sometimes only the top was worn over a cotton print dress in a less formal manner, the skirt being omitted.

There is a strong conservative bent on the Mescalero Reservation: most, if not all, males and females undergo traditional puberty ceremonies, the native language is widely used, and other traditional practices and attitudes are staunchly maintained. Mrs. Hugar importantly notes that definite traditional styles of the girl's Na-i-es garment and its elaboration follow along band lines, and that respective types are recognizable. This is borne out by the examination of dresses in historic photographs. For example, one Chiricahua style of yoke is decorated with a dense, closely attached, curving row of metal cones across the front and back. Structurally, and even decoratively, the Derby Dress is very similar to a number of other examples in public and private collections that are known to be Apache. But it is difficult to determine the time lapse from the date of their manufacture to the present. Temporal distance impedes verification of tribal and band attribution.

Studying Jicarilla Apache women in historic photographs reveals that their band's styles of skin dress is closely related to garments of the closely allied Ute tribe. A specifically shaped, yellow-painted yoke, typically bordered with lazystitched lanes of black and white seed beads, is worn over a separate skin or cloth dress. These yokes bear little resemblance to the Derby dress or to Apache garments further to the south and west. Therefore, it is doubtful that the Derby ensemble is of Jicarilla origin. Styles change, and the Derby dress is possibly an archaic Eastern Apache form. The garment exhibits all the characteristics of the first half of the nineteenth century, as is the documented example in the Berlandier Collection.

MOCCASINS

Another poignant clue that the Derby dress is

Apache is the accompanying pair of slipper-type moccasins. In the Lino Sanchez y Tapia watercolors illustrating the Berlandier journal, the moccasins worn by the three Lipan, Comanche, and Cocos women are low-cut rather than high-top "boot-moccasins." The Derby moccasins are of an Apache style prevalent at least into the late nineteenth century, although this low-cut type is considered to have been for men in later times. These moccasins have a separate, pointed-toe sole of tanned skin, and a triangular-shaped insert, both sewn in place with sinew. The point of the elongated insert extends from the foot opening almost to the tips of the toes, dividing the instep of the upper. Each stitch of the inside seam carries a white pony bead. The outside seam of the insert has a doubled welt cut into fringes. Part of the insert corresponds to a tongue and extends well beyond the moccasin opening. It can be folded forward to a point even with the base of the wearer's toes.

The points that cut into the hide across the straight leading edge of the tongue insert are significant. Each point is supplied with a short, doubled thong skewered through the tip in the same manner as the similar points on the skirt. A doubled welt is sewn into the heel seam and cut into fringes. The top edge of the opening is cut into points around its perimeter. Even though the moccasins are soiled and heavily worn, it is evident that the powdered red ochre paint that colors them perfectly matches that of the dress. In addition, the identical character of the points cut into the tongue incontrovertibly indicates that the moccasins were made to complete the ensemble.

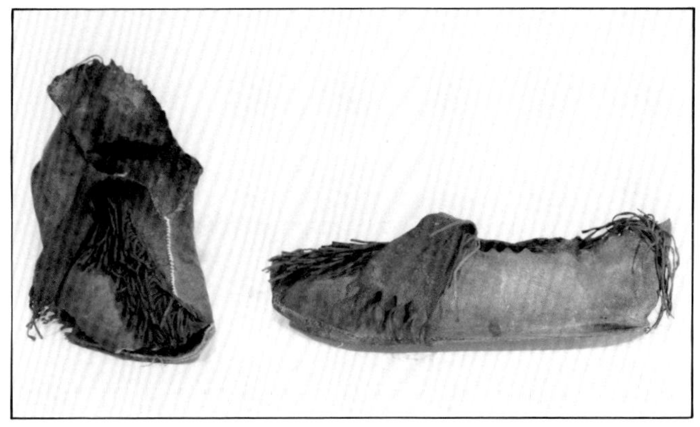

Figure 21. Moccasins, Apache type, ca. 1850.

If these moccasins are indeed of Apache origin, as are the similar dresses with which this fine ensemble has been compared, then tribal attribution of the dress is likewise certain. Certainly the dress exhibits strong Apache character. It is probably of a style that has rudimentary aspects of later styles, but it is of such an archaic nature that it no longer resembles reservation period or contemporary dresses closely enough to ascertain the maker's band affiliation. Additional research may reveal the band origin and other pertinent data about this remarkable suit of clothing.

ACKNOWLEDGMENTS

For their assistance, appreciation is extended to: Dr. John Ewers, Jonathan Batkin, Robert Gilmore, Elbys Hugar, Judy Jordan, Rose and Dennis Lessard, Rex and Ginger Reddick, and Edson Way.

A Pipe in the Derby Collection

Benson L. Lanford

Many of the stone bowls and wooden stems of Native American pipes from the Great Lakes, Prairie, and Northern Plains are remarkable for their artistry, either bold in their simplicity or striking in their complexity. The bowls may be austere, stylized, or display involved carving, with inlay of contrasting stone or lead. Stems can be pierced, painted, carved, branded, brass-tacked, inlaid with metal, and wrapped with fur, birdskin, porcupine quillwork, or beadwork. Assorted feathers, ribbons, and hair are used as streamers to further bedeck the stems. The custom of smoking, for pleasure or ceremony, was widespread throughout the Americas, but the area cultures mentioned above produced the most elaborate devices to facilitate the practice, raising smoking paraphernalia to a high art.

The ceremonial pipestems of a certain genre are each contradictory within themselves. A third or half of the length toward the mouthpiece received elaborate attention, but the remaining portion was left starkly plain in contrast. This undecorated section may provoke *horror vacui* in some beholders, which may have led to the curious existence of a number of atypical pipestems with the usually plain wooden area toward the bowl fancifully painted. Actually, a pipestem with bowl illustrated in Dockstader's *Indian Art of the Americas,*[1] and several stems in the University of Philadelphia Museum collections, fit this description. At one time the latter were owned by the renowned artist, George Catlin, after whom catlinite, the predominant mineral used for the manufacture of pipebowls, was named.

Catlin collected numerous specimens from the Northern Plains and Upper Missouri River tribes during his sojurn there in the early 1830s. Subsequently, in unsuccessful business ventures in this country and Europe, he lectured and displayed his "Indian Gallery," as he deemed his assemblage of paintings and artifacts. For an extended time, Catlin sought to have the United States Government purchase his collection, but after continued financial failure in Europe, it was sold at auction to an American businessman. Time and the elements ravaged the objects; however, some of theme were ultimately acquired by the University Museum and the Smithsonian Institution. There is no way to know how many items collected by Catlin were scattered, their history lost.

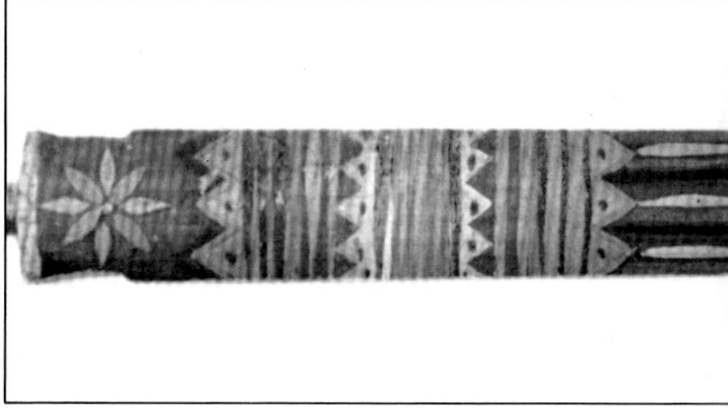

Figure 22. Close-up of painted design on pipe.

In *Indian Art In Pipestone, George Catlin's Portfolio In The British Museum,* editor John Ewers states, "All ordinary Indian pipe stems have a division more or less distant from the pipe. That portion nearest to the bowl, called by the Indians 'the shoulder,' is never covered: the wood being bare, and often curiously carved, or ornamented with figures burned in with a heated iron. The other half of the stem, which is covered with braids of porcupine quills or other ornaments, is called 'the body' of the pipe, and the ornamental covering is called the 'dress.'"[2] The nine flat pipestems drawn by Catlin in two plates in his *Portfolio* have embellishments in the form of geometric arrangements, with human and animal forms drawn on the "shoulder" of each in a most un-Indian-like style. It would be interesting to compare the numerous pipes illustrated in Catlin's paintings and drawings to determine how many of them he elaborated in a like manner.

It is certain that some objects in Catlin's collection have been enhanced, most likely by his own hand. It is probable that he even combined and entirely invented a number of articles as well. Indeed, the pipestems from the Catlin collection in the University Museum have all had the traditionally unelaborated wooden sections painted with a solid background and naive, "Indianesque" designs in what appear to be oil paints. Likewise, in the collections of the Smithsonian, there is a Great Lakes style wooden cradleboard with motifs painted to emulate

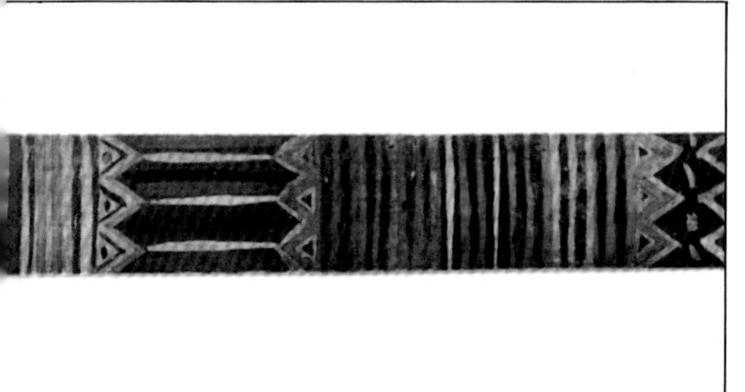

Indian ornamentation. An accompanying doll with no relationship to Indian examples has a disproportionately large, grotesque, painted plaster head, and its stubby body is merely a length of square-cut lumber covered with cradle wrappings. This cradleboard and doll, too, had been in the Catlin collection. The board itself was surely altered from its original state after it left Indian hands, and the doll is assuredly a non-Indian contrivance.

The Derby Collection boasts a fine Northern Plains quilled pipestem with a handsome lead-inlaid bowl, dating from the early nineteenth century. Collection history indicates that this pipe was submitted to auction from an old New England estate whose owners had collected American Indian artifacts. The usually plain portion of the stem has been completely painted, top, shoulders and bottom, with a series of adjacent bands of complex designs which resemble quillwork patterns. Rather generous amounts of oil paints were used, the brush strokes and paint noticeably similar to those of the modified pipes and the cradleboard described above. The designs, however, are less spontaneous, more carefully conceived and more intricate. A greater variety of colors was utilized by the unknown hand to fill in the undeveloped zone of the stem in non-Indian character. It is certainly possible that the alteration of this pipestem was done by George Catlin himself in an effort to hyperbolize what was already superlative. Additional analysis and comparison must be done to attain a trustworthy judgement to this prospect; the possibility is intriguing!

A Rare Apache Medicine Bag

Jonathan Batkin

For most Americans the name Apache conjures images of Geronimo and his band of Chiricahuas. For those familiar with Native American arts, the name is most often associated with the master basketweavers of Arizona—the groups called Western Apaches. Many don't realize that Apaches were among the first nomadic Plains Indians encountered living in tipis and hunting buffalo by Coronado's expedition in 1540. By the middle of the nineteenth century, only one Apache group still lived exclusively on the Plains. These were the Kiowa-Apaches, who had banded together with the Kiowas in the eighteenth century. Three other groups still ventured onto the Plains at least occasionally at that time: the Jicarilla Apaches of northern New Mexico, the Mescalero Apaches of south central New Mexico, and the Lipan Apaches of Texas.

Aside from basketry, Apache arts are poorly known, and the only thorough study to date is *Western Apache Material Culture,* edited by Alan Ferg (1987). Apache arts are not rare, but few systematic collections exist; thus our understanding of them is based on documented artifacts scattered far and wide in the world's museums. Those widely dispersed objects provide the clues that identify the medicine bag that we discuss here.

The technology of making painted rawhide containers, or parfleches, as they are popularly known, is believed to have evolved from the making of bark containers. The evolution of painted rawhide is also believed to have occurred within historic times. Facts that support these beliefs are: that the use of painted rawhide containers is associated principally with the use of the European-introduced horse; that many Plains dwellers were originally Woodlands dwellers who were displaced by the encroachment of Europeans; and that the oldest known techniques for decorating rawhide (incising and scraping) are traditional Woodlands techniques for decorating bark.

The earliest accounts of Plains Indians—descriptions of Apaches encountered by Coronado's and others' expeditions—support these beliefs. Though the accounts include detailed descriptions of tanned hides used for tipis and clothing, of weapons, and of the gear used on dogs (the beasts of burden before the horse), they lack any mention of rawhide containers.

By the nineteenth century, all but the Western Apaches made parfleches. The Kiowa-Apaches presumably made parfleches that resembled Kiowa types, but documented examples are rare. The remaining groups—Jicarilla, Mescalero, Chiricahua, and Lipan—made a variety of parfleches resembling types made by peoples of the Plains, Plateau, and Great Basin. The documentation is scant and varies from one group to the next, so group styles cannot all be clearly defined. Nevertheless, an outline of Apache parfleche styles is possible, and a brief sketch will help us understand the Derby medicine bag. In the interests of simplicity, I will refer to examples published in Mable Morrow's readily available book, *Indian Rawhide: An American Folk Art.* Although some Apache parfleches in her book are attributed rather than documented examples, they are excellent, typical examples.

The large, folding, envelope-like bag that we often view as the Plains "suitcase," used to store clothing, dried meat, and other goods, and often carried on a travois or lashed to a packsaddle, was certainly made by the Jicarilla and Mescalero Apaches. Jicarilla examples are extremely large, and most examples are decorated with variations of only a few designs. One of the most conspicuous design characteristics is the outlining of large elements with a profusion of small triangles. A detail from a fine example in the Taylor Museum is reproduced by Morrow (1975: 59,85), who mistakenly stated its location as the Denver Art Museum.

The Mescalero style of the large envelope is quite beautiful, and is a more typical size for this type of bag. A detail of an example at the Museum of the American Indian has been published (Morrow 1975:59). Mescalero parfleches commonly have finely detailed elements in black and red that appear to be deliberate representations of hide thongs with tin cones: a line or elongated triangle in one of the colors is tipped with a dot or a short isosceles triangle in the other color. This design element is so common, and Apache clothing so often has fine fringes with tin cones, that the similarity can hardly be coincidental. Another detail that can be found in many Mescalero parfleches is the incision of parts of the design. The designs are not scraped or excised, as on early Plateau parfleches, but some portions of outlines are cut, rather than drawn.

Whether or not the Chiricahuas made these is still unclear to me. I have seen examples attributed to them or to "Arizona Apaches," but have not yet encountered a well-documented example. The Chiricahuas may very well have made them, because there are many envelopes that are clearly Apache, but that do not resemble Jicarilla or Mescalero types.

Cylindrical headdress cases and short cylindrical feather cases were also made. The former are similar in all respects except painted designs to other Plains headdress cases. Documented Jicarilla examples are known, and their designs are generally what one finds on half of a large envelope. The small feather cases are as short as six inches in length. The few I have seen were alike, but the only documented example was Mescalero.

The Derby parfleche is one of eleven examples of its type known to me in museums and private collections. Again, in almost all respects except surface decoration, it resembles a standard parfleche type of the Plains, Plateau, and Great Basin. Examples from all these areas are either square (or nearly so) or are rectangular with their greatest dimension measured along the horizontal axis. They have fringes hanging from their vertical sides that, in some cases, are quite long. They are well documented as men's containers for personal medicines, and many photographs from the turn of the century show them hanging on tripods outside their owners' tipis. They were often made in pairs, although there is no evidence that Apaches made them any way but singly. This type of parfleche should not be confused with similar bags that lack fringes, generally documented as women's bags for keeping tools, paints, or the like. These, too, were made throughout the areas mentioned, as well as by Apaches.

Only a few Apache parfleches of the type in the Derby Collection have reliable documentation that dates to the time of collection. The best-documented example is Lipan Apache and is now in the British Museum. It was collected by Captain J. A. Wilcox, 4th Cavalry, on May 19, 1873, when General Ranald Mackenzie violated international law and crossed the Mexican border to raid an encampment of Lipans and Kickapoos. This parfleche has been published (Coe 1976:218). A documented example in the Museum of the American Indian (catalog number 16/1329) was originally in the collection of Major John Gregory Bourke, the meticulous researcher and amateur ethnographer. Bourke recorded it as Lipan Apache and gave its origin as Texas, but the circumstances under which he acquired it are unknown.

Another parfleche of this type was collected for the Historical Society of New Mexico at Jemez Pueblo in 1886, and is now at the Laboratory of Anthropology in Santa Fe (catalog number 24803/12). It has as its principal design a large hourglass figure in red and green outlined in black; the hourglass is free-floating on an unpainted ground. A small pinwheel-like element is in each corner of the hourglass. This parfleche is certainly of Apache origin, and was documented as a medicine bag (talega) when it was collected.

Almost all of the known parfleches of this type have bilaterally symmetrical designs divided vertically by a narrow panel of repeating motifs. An outer border of alternating black and white squares is common; on the Derby parfleche, the outer border is lacking, but two rows of alternating squares, suggesting a checkerboard, divide the main design field. Many of these parfleches have hourglass shapes painted on them, either as major designs or as smaller motifs. Many also have pinwheels that are either painted or painted and incised. More often than not, the pinwheels are on the top flap, and not the front of the bag: the Derby and Laboratory of Anthropology examples are exceptions.

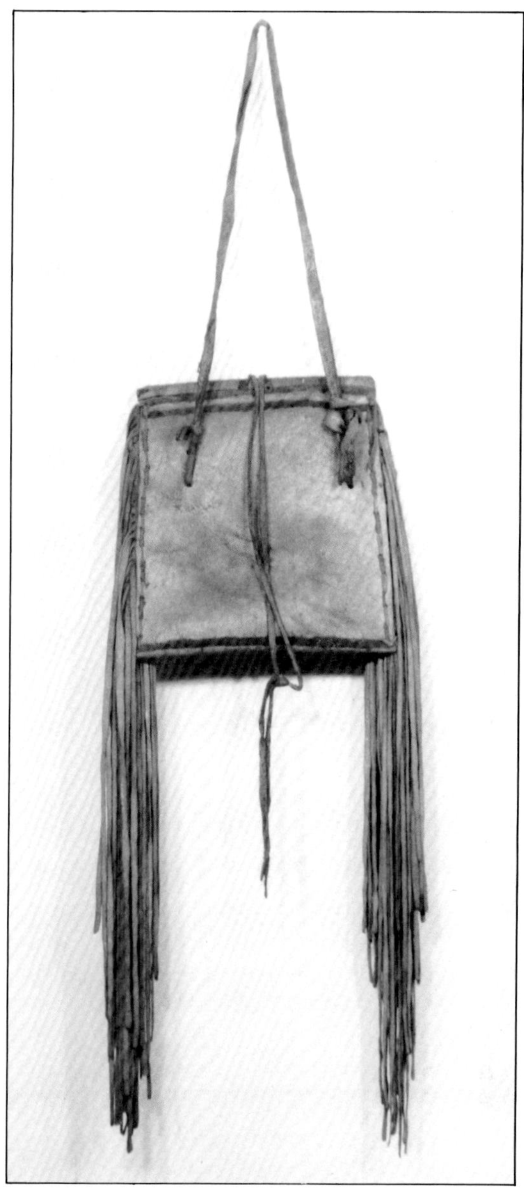

Figure 23. Back of pouch (See color plate 13 for front)

Both this type of bag and the large Jicarilla Apache envelope are similar to parfleches of the Plateau peoples. The Jicarilla Apache parfleches resemble those of the Kutenai, Umatilla, Yakima, and Klickitat. Of particular interest are painted fringelike borders on large motifs and painted designs on the inner flaps of the parfleches. The reader can compare a Kutenai parfleche in the Taylor Museum, illustrated by Morrow (1975:64), with the Taylor Museum's Jicarilla parfleche mentioned previously (Morrow 1975:59). Although painted designs of both regions are similar, the Jicarilla Apache parfleches are much larger than those of the other peoples.

The Apache medicine bag in the Derby Collection is also similar to Plateau types. Few of these parfleches have been published, but those that have bear similarities in overall design, as well as in details such as painted "fringes" and bordering bands of alternating dark and light squares or rectangles (Morrow 1975:128, 203). According to James A. Teit, these parfleches were used and traded widely among Salish peoples. He states that the Okanagon made them in large numbers and traded them to the Kamloops and others; but at the same time, the Okanagon acquired them in trade from the Kalispel and other tribes (1909:498; 1930:221).

Influences on material culture due to the migration and contact of peoples are common. This medicine bag in the Derby Collection is certainly an example, although the events are impossible to reconstruct. The Apaches are linguistically distinct from the Salish and they migrated from the Northwest before adopting the technology of making parfleches. Therefore, the movement of other peoples must account for the similarities. Some scholars have attributed similar phenomena to the migration of the Numic-speaking peoples of the Great Basin—the region that forms a corridor between the Plateau and the Southwest—and this appears to be the most logical explanation for the similarities in parfleche design.

Unfortunately for our purposes, parfleches from the Great Basin are quite rare. Published examples are superficially similar to those of the Plateau peoples and Apaches (Fowler and Matley 1979:173-178), but so few exist that a Great Basin style is not evident. Perhaps further research will provide the pieces necessary to complete the puzzle.

In summary, we can say that the Derby parfleche is a typical but early example of a rare type. Its construction is the same as all other examples. The body of the bag is a single piece of rawhide, folded at the bottom and again at the top, and laced together at the sides. The fringe at each side is composed of two large panels of hide. Each panel was sliced through its entire length except for about one inch at one end. The one-inch length preserved on each panel was sandwiched between the front and back of the parfleche and laced into it. Unlike the fringes on many other examples, none on the Derby parfleche are scalloped—a treatment that links these parfleches to other Apache artifacts such as saddlebags.

The parfleche is painted red, green, and dark brown. The design, which incorporates two large, negative, hourglass shapes, is bilaterally symmetrical and divided by a checkerboard design. Four pinwheels are on the horizontal axis of the design; another pair is on the flap of the bag, flanking its center. As mentioned, the bag is uncharacteristic for its lack of a border design around the edges; instead, the design extends past the laces.

Many of these parfleches are painted in a much wider range of colors; as many as six colors occur on some. Many are also painted more precisely than the Derby example. The only other bags I have examined with this coloration were also painted in an archaic style. I believe that they are all very old, probably dating to 1850 or earlier.

We may never fully understand the significance of this great artifact, but we can admire it as a beautiful example from a great tradition of abstract painting.

Kiowa Belt Pouches in the Derby Collection

David Wooley

By the 1700s, the Kiowa occupied an area of the Southern Plains, bordered on the west by New Mexico, and extending south to Mexico, and north into Kansas. The Kiowa were of the general Plains culture-type, in that they were nomadic bison hunters and horse pastoralists who spent most of the year living in small bands. During the classic Plains period (1775-1875), Kiowa men gained recognition through war exploits, political ability, generosity, or spiritual attainment (Mayhall, 1971).

All young women were taught the basic skills required to make and maintain clothing, to tan hides, and to provide the necessities of life. As Schneider (1983) points out, "Kiowa women, unlike men, achieved recognition for their skills in craftwork" (p. 236). Twelve of the twenty-five most famous men among the Kiowa in the last quarter of the nineteenth century had spouses who were known for their skill in the construction of tipis, saddles, and beadwork. Three women, in particular, were recognized as being outstanding beadworkers. They were Mawkonty, Kotedayty, and Saubeodle (Mishkin, 1940; Schneider, 1983).

KIOWA BEADWORK

It has been suggested by some that, because Southern Plains Indian tribes such as the Kiowa had no tradition of quillwork embroidery, the natural outcome was to use a minimum of beadwork to carry the aesthetic impact of the object. Certainly the Kiowas must have had a longstanding tradition of using paint to cover the surface of clothing, as well as other objects, both sacred and secular. Indeed, a great part of the visual impact of Kiowa art is carried by the use of applied color, both for overall surface decoration and for highlighting various portions of an object. In addition, the use of fringe—either straight, finely twisted (or in some cases, twisted cotton cordage), or dyed—is a part of the aesthetic appeal of Kiowa art (Conn, 1979, 1976; Hail, 1983, Schneider, 1983).

The Kiowa use of metal further enhances the objects. Metal may include tin cones added to fringe, and German silver or nickel conchos or buttons. Each of these decorative techniques transforms the object they embellish from mere two-dimensional items (especially when they were worn) into three-dimensional sculptural art forms. These objects possess a beauty and quality not unlike that of a contemporary mobile (Wooley, 1986).

The Southern Plains tribes appear to have had a long tradition of using yellow and green paint, especially to decorate their clothing, tipis, and other objects. Debate continues whether certain objects are of Kiowa or Comanche manufacture. Generally, the Comanche employed simple designs and fewer colors. The Kiowas, on the other hand, employed less white, and used more elaborate color combinations (Schneider, 1983).

The Kiowa often have white, outlined, geometric designs, with several different colors used to outline a pattern (Conn, 1976; Schneider, 1983). This creates an internal complexity of design without clutter. The Kiowa seemed to believe that a design should stand out in contrast to its background, with light color used to outline designs on dark grounds, and vice versa (Schneider, 1983).

The design variation on Kiowa beadwork is so great that identical or similar designs are rarely found. Schneider (1983) observed this design variation in Kiowa cradleboards:

> "This variation provides some insight into Kiowa beadwork traditions. A design belonged to the woman who originated it and could be used by others only with her permission. Some designs were handed down in families and became associated with certain family traditions. However, there was also a strong emphasis on originality of design and on creating new designs; even family designs were not repeated in exactly the same manner, and there was a constant search for inspiration for new designs." (pp. 310-311.)

The Kiowa decorative preference leaned toward delicate ornament rather than appliquéd or embroidered beadwork. The tendency was to confine beadwork to narrow edgings and light

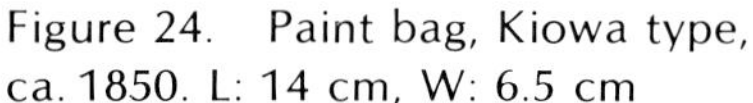

Figure 24. Paint bag, Kiowa type, ca. 1850. L: 14 cm, W: 6.5 cm

Figure 25. Strike-a-light, Kiowa type, ca. 1850. L: 17.5 cm, W: 8:2 cm

Figure 26. Strike-a-light, Kiowa type, ca. 1850. L: 12 cm, W: 6.5 cm

trims. Additionally, another characteristic of Kiowa beadwork is the prevalence of linear design elements.

In many of the Kiowa objects that are fully beaded, the linear design elements are presented in a vertical pattern or a series of stacked designs that tend to lead the eye in a vertical path. Seldom are the designs done in a horizontal fashion, perhaps with the exception of dresses for females. The propensity for vertical, linear designs is undoubtedly a product of construction; however, it is also set by artistic preference and the fact that attached elements—such as leather fringes, beaded strings, or bone hair pipes—influence the artist's decisions about spatial arrangement.

A DISCUSSION OF KIOWA BELT BAGS

Kiowa belt sets (strike-a-lights, awl cases, whetstone cases) are among the few objects manufactured by the Kiowa in which the majority, if not all, of the surface is beaded. Cradleboards, mirror bags,[1] and occasionally, men's moccasins, are the only other material culture items that the Kiowa would decorate with significant quantities of beads. Items such as moccasins, leggings, shirts, and dresses generally display a minimum of applied beadwork decoration.

Today, when American Indian objects are written about, frequently the approach is to discuss the chronological development of object types, beadwork designs, aesthetics, or technical aspects of applied decoration. Seldom is mention made in today's literature of the object's actual, technological use within the culture that produced it.

In this case, it is rarely recognized that strike-a-lights, awl cases, whetstone cases, and knife sheaths—often attached in some manner to a belt or other object—constitute a portion of a female's or male's tool kit,and as such represent a portion of that individual's or culture's technology. Certainly, as objects made to hold

Figure 27. Strike-a-light and awl case, Kiowa type, ca. 1860.
Strike-a-light — L: 15.5 cm (excluding drops), Max W: 9 cm
Awl case — L: 19 cm (excluding drops), W: 2 cm

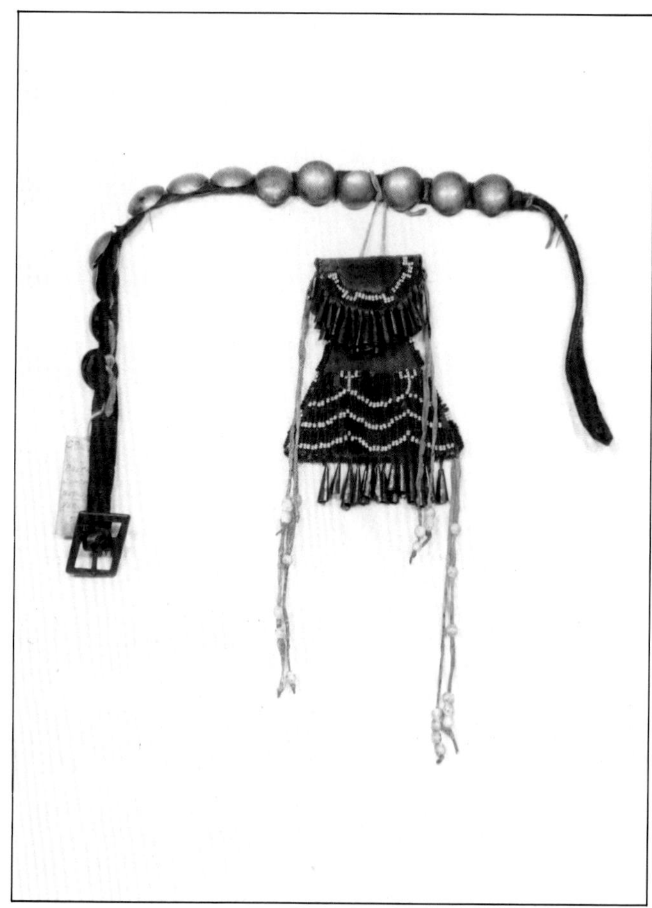

Figure 28. Strike-a-light, Kiowa type, ca. 1860. L: 13 cm, Max. W: 9 cm

and carry tools, they are very specialized containers.

From a functional standpoint, these tools could have been carried in a single container, rather than in the individual cases that were manufactured, and there was absolutely no practical reason for applying decoration to the surface of these containers. Decoration did not make it easier for one to extract tools from their containers, nor did it add to the longevity of the object. On the contrary, it weakens the leather.

It has generally been assumed that belt tool kits (strike-a-lights, whetstone cases, awl cases) were used by women only. "Kiowa women had matched sets of small pouches in which they kept such tools as whetstones, firesteels, etc," (Conn, 1976). These containers (for all Plains tribes) have often been shown with belts decorated with German or nickel silver.[2] These belt sets are also seen in miniature, as part of a doll's clothing.[3] Yet, it has not been brought to the public's attention—although there is ample evidence—that these tool kits were carried by men as well as women, and were as much a part of male paraphernalia as they were women's equipment. They are commonly seen attached to bow and quiver cases. Strike-a-lights appear frequently in historic photographs, especially early photographs of Southern Plains men.[4] If they appeared only in photographs, one might make the assumption that tool kits were merely props, but they also appear with males in pictographic ledger art.[5]

KIOWA STRIKE-A-LIGHTS IN THE DERBY COLLECTION

The Derby Kiowa strike-a-light collection can be separated into three categories. The first category may be identified primarily by the object's age, simple design characteristics, and basic rectangular shape. The second category is

Figure 29. Strike-a-light, Kiowa type, ca. 1860. L: 16 cm, Max. W: 9 cm

again marked by the object's age, more complicated yet delicate designs, and trapezoidal shape. The third category is marked by a change in beadwork application, from more or less horizontal rows of beads applied in a lazystitch technique, to wide single strings of beads applied vertically as well as horizontally. (A category not represented in the Derby Collection is a Kiowa-Comanche strike-a-light, in which the beadwork is done in a peyote or brick stitch technique.[6])

The first category of strike-a-lights, or tool kits, in the Derby Collection may represent some of the earliest Southern Plains beadwork, quite probably pre-1860. The belt bags are very similar in shape (Figures 24, 25, 26), a basic rectangle with right angle corners. Two bags (Figures 24, 25) have only two bead colors: a translucent red (often referred to as Kiowa red), and opaque white. Figure 26 contains a third bead color, blue. The designs are quite simple, with solid design patterns either in red or white. The minimal use of color and color choices provides sharp visual contrasts. Figure 26 is characteristic of and compares favorably to them.

Perhaps the most aesthetically interesting of these three belt bags is a pony beaded bag that contains vermillion powder (Figure 24). It was originally purchased with an awl case, a skirt, and yoke (the skirt and yoke are undoubtedly Apache rather than Kiowa). The designs on the body of this pouch present a vibrating positive and negative spatial play and the vertical nature of the design elements leads the viewer's eyes directly to the flap. The flap displays two white dots on a translucent red beaded field that peer back at you as if they were eyes illuminated in the dark.

The second category of belt pouches in the Derby Collection is represented by examples that are from the 1860s and 1870s (Figures 29-31). Aesthetically, all of the examples in this group are quite remarkable. All are trapezoidal in form and have more than two bead colors. The makers employ twisted fringe with or without German silver wrapping, or have bead string drops from the corners of the bag. Most examples use either a German silver button or harness leather spots on the flap.

Of particular note in this grouping is a strike-a-light and awl case (Figure 27) collected by George Dillwyn Cook, a graduate of Maine Medical College and an agency doctor for the government, who was in Indian territory between 1866 and 1869. The design element found on the bottom of the pouch employs a motif common to many Kiowa strike-a-lights. The design appears as a series of shallow triangles or a zig-zag pattern. The face of the bag is vertically separated by two lines of white beads that outline a rectangular design. The center features a series of stacked squares. The strong visual appeal of this and other Kiowa strike-a-lights is achieved by the use of the dark red beads as a background, with stark contrast provided by white beads that outline subtle colors, especially a variety of blue beads. Also—as is common with many of the Kiowa strike-a-lights—the reverse side of the bag is partially beaded. In this case, the artist has

Figure 30. Strike-a-light, Kiowa type, ca. 1860.
L: 14 cm, Max. W: 9 cm

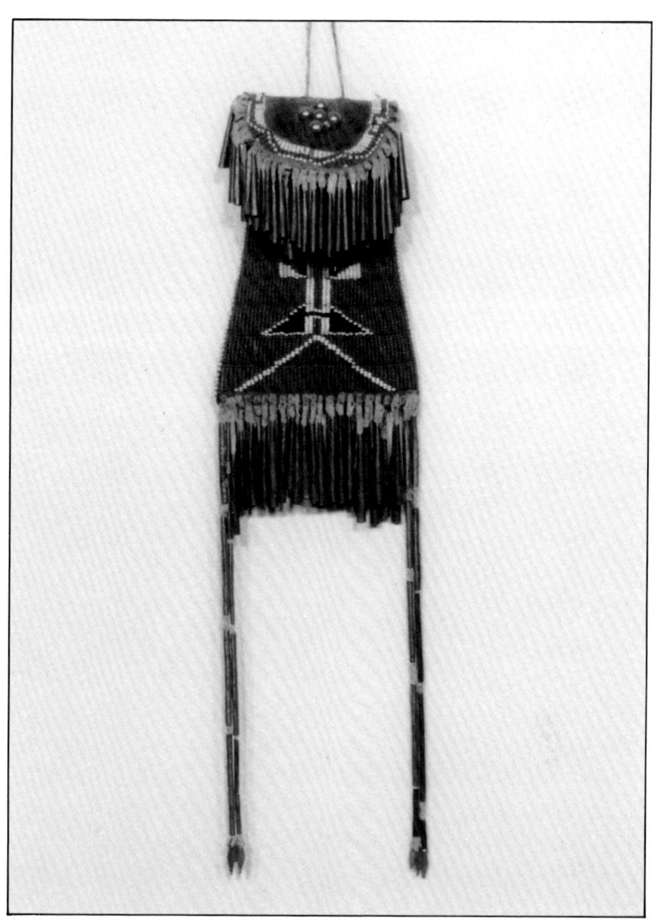

Figure 31. Strike-a-light, Kiowa type, ca. 1860.
L: 18 cm, Max. W: 9.2 cm

returned to only two bead colors, opaque white and translucent blue. The sense and use of positive and negative space on this bag is wonderful. The awl case that accompanies this strike-a-light displays a common solution to the problem of adding designs to the surface of such a small object—that is, the stacking of diamonds outlined with white beads.

Figures 28, 30 and 31 are also worthy of special attention. All three of these examples display a more delicate, less blocky approach to the design elements, especially in the beadwork designs found on the flaps. These pouches use three or more bead colors, and the delicate nature of the patterns are reminiscent of the designs found on the single lanes of beadwork found on Kiowa men's and women's moccasins. These designs take on the appearance of zippers on clothing.

The pouch (Figure 30) is unusual in that the design is carried horizontally, with the gold white outlining separating the beadwork on the lower part of the bag into three horizontal planes, rather than the strong vertical nature of the other example. Figure 31 is an excellent example of Kiowa color preference, with Kiowa or trader blue as the predominate color. This strike-a-light was collected at Anadarko, Oklahoma, with a German silver-decorated harness leather belt and a whetstone case that was decorated with peyote stitched beadwork. Some of the design elements in this particular strike-a-light are reminiscent of Cheyenne, Sioux, and other Plains nation strike-a-lights.

One strike-a-light (Illustration No. 44) fits in the category of Kiowa strike-a-lights in which the beadwork is applied in long lines of horizontal and vertical beads, with a white line of beads outlining the triangles and circles and—as is typical with this style of belt bag—a second outlining color. However, the beadwork on the back of this example employs the more typical lines of lazystitch beadwork. This methodology of bead application and the appearance of the designs is reminiscent of the Crows' and other inter-mountain groups' approach to bead application, color, and design choices. The Kiowa maintained a close association with the Crows, who were their neighbors prior to the Kiowa's move to the southern plains. Yet, if one might point to an influence in the technical and aesthetic approach to these strike-a-lights and also to Kiowa cradle boards, the source would probably be the Prairie and/or Southeastern tribes—many of whom by 1860 were residing near the Kiowa in Oklahoma territory. The awl case that was collected with this strike-a-light is a delightful object. The beadwork on the body of the awl case is applied in a barber pole design, employing five different colors.

I have chosen not to enter into a debate here as to whether all of these red and blue background strike-a-lights, awl cases, and whetstone cases were made by the Kiowa or the Comanche. Suffice it to say that at this time I firmly believe that they are of Kiowa origin. However, I hope this is not the final word; I welcome evidence and debate to the contrary. I also feel that further research with historic photographs such as that done by Bill Holms (1985), could provide some new insights.

Significant discussions of Southern Plains beadwork are sorely lacking in the available literature. Southern Plains nations have earned their rightful place in this nation's cultural heritage, and deserve the recognition of their artistic contributions, past and present. And, as is too often the case, we ignore those continuing traditions. Belt sets are still an important part of the traditional Kiowa dress, as can be seen in a photo of Sugar Kalaukarty taken at Anadarko, Oklahoma, in 1971 (Schneider, 1983).

If anything can sum up Kiowa beadwork and Kiowa belt sets, it is Dick Conn's (1976) statement that the Kiowa were "a people who were essentially miniaturists in beading," (p. 84).

Belt Pouches in the Derby Collection

Benson L. Lanford

A belt pouch with a long triangular flap covering the opening and pouch front was in use among a number of northern and central Plains tribes during the nineteenth century. Four examples in the Derby Collection are discussed in this article; three for adults and one for a child. Extant pouches of this type are rare. Indeed, few collections have even a single specimen. The earliest of these are decorated with pony beads. Some exhibit both pony and seed beads, and many are elaborated totally with seed beads. Few triangular flap belt pouches are decorated with porcupine quillwork. Documentation is scarce; however, two pouches were sketched by Rudolph Friederich Kurz in about 1851.[1] One has a row of diamonds down the middle of the flap, a common motif to be discussed later, and the other a triangle, diamond, and zigzag arrangement. Only a single historic photograph of a person wearing this type of belt pouch has been found. Julius Meyer, "Indian interpreter, Trader and Dealer in Indian, Chinese and Japanese Curiosities, 170 Farnham Street; Omaha, Nebraska," was photographed in the company of Sitting Bull (an Oglala, not the famous Hunkpapa Chief), Red Cloud (Oglala), and Swift Bear and Spotted Tail (both Brule) in 1875 in Omaha, Nebraska by F. F. Currier.[2] The flap of the pouch worn by Meyer is rounded, a variant of the more typical pointed flap style. A very similar pouch is in the Smithsonian Institution (collection number 154033). A distinctive belt pouch type with a rounded flap the same size and shape as the pouch itself was popular in Montana and in the Plateau region.

The triangular flap belt pouch is typically made of buffalo hide and measures an average of 4″ by 3½″. A triangular extension of the back folds over the top, covers the opening and hangs to a point well below the pouch bottom margin. The front of this flap is covered with pony or seed beadwork in a variety of techniques, particularly "lazystitch," "Crow stitch" and/or "overlay." Edge beadwork in a number of "picot" or "running lazystitch" configurations is common on the flap borders. A few pouches have a combination of both bead types, indicating the period of transition from the predominant use of pony beads to seed bead use from approximately 1860 to 1875. If there is any beadwork on the pouch itself, it is usually a lane of lazystitch covering the outer margin seams. A separate leather belt is sewn to the back. This is usually long enough to tie, leaving the often-decorated ends pendant.

Documented examples of triangular flap belt pouches exist from the Sioux, Assiniboin, Crow, Cheyenne and Blackfoot. Pouches with beadwork characteristic of the Ute, Fort Balknap Gros Ventre, and Assiniboin have been observed. The Blackfoot produced examples of these belt pouches as late as the turn of the century, often as one of a variety of types for women's belt sets. Only the Sioux, however, continued making them into the twentieth century, and the genre itself was always most prevalent in this tribe.

The three adult size Derby pouches are made of native-tanned buffalo hide beaded on the flesh side. The naturally dark epidermis is evident inside and underneath the flap of each pouch. The child's pouch appears to be of native-tanned steer hide.

The first triangular flap belt pouch in the Derby Collection (Figure 32) came with a group of beadwork collected mainly from the Cheyenne in 1864 by James B. Beard, who worked on the construction of the Union Pacific Railroad under Grenville M. Dodge, for whom Dodge City, Kansas, was named. A note written by Beard and found with the pouch states, "This beadwork was done by the Indian squaws many years ago. I got it from them in 1864." Beard had had a number of skirmishes with the Indians when he operated a business hauling lumber to Denver in the 1860s. Since this was primarily Cheyenne and Arapaho country at that time, it is possible that this pouch was produced by one of those two tribes, even though aspects of the beadwork are not dissimilar from Sioux art.

This is the only Derby pouch with the triangular flap cut separately from and sewn to the pouch. Like the child's size pouch, it has a belt

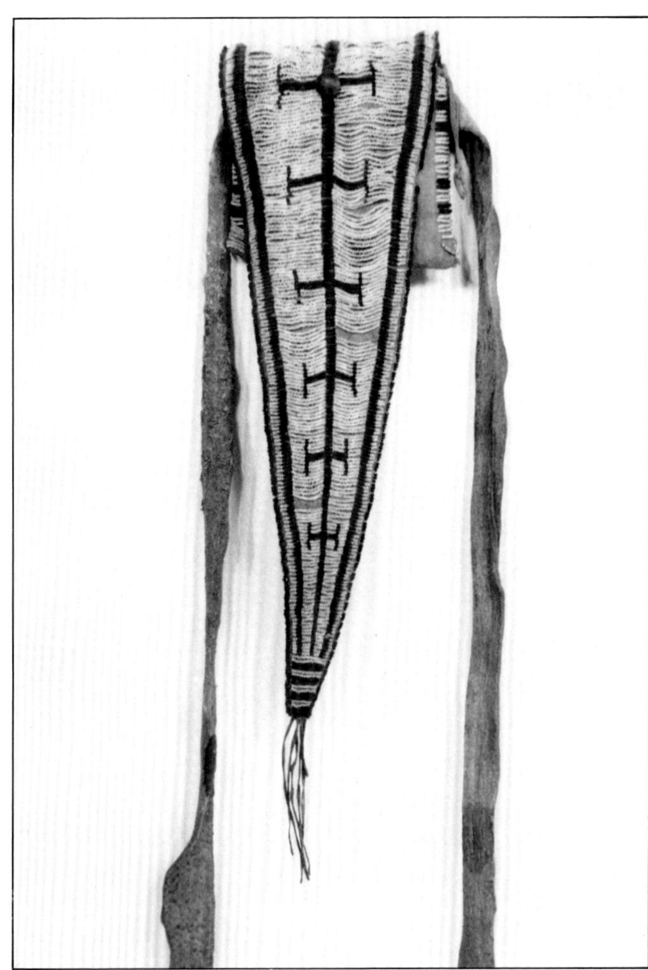

Figure 32. Triangular flap belt pouch, Cheyenne type, ca. 1860.
L: 33 cm, Max. W: 11 cm

attached to the top of the pouch back. However, the epidermis has been completely removed from the belt of this first example.

The flap of the belt pouch collected by Beard is decorated with fine seed beads, the white background executed in "Crow stitch," and the green cross bars formed by simply changing bead color. Medium-dark transparent green and white-lined red beads in lazystitch create the linear motifs. The edge finish is running lazystitch, averaging three black beads per stitch. The meticulous execution of the beadwork is evident in the carefully tapered outer green stripes which are outlined with a narrow red line. The central solid green stripe is also tapered. A lane of white and black beads lazystitched on the outer edges is the only decoration on the pouch proper. A thong doubled through the flap ties to a brass button on the pouch front to close the opening. A num-

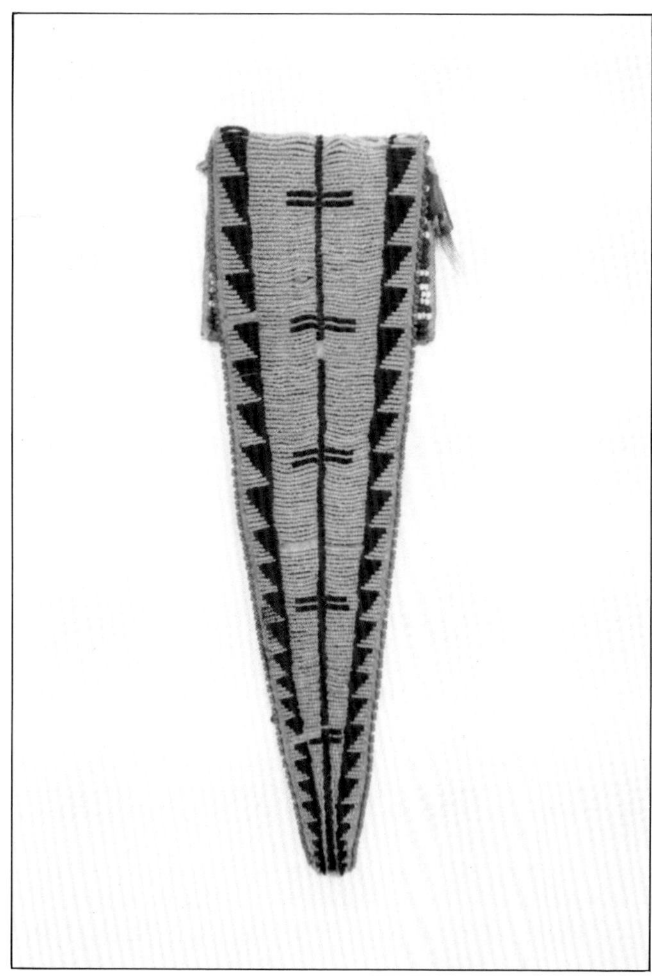

Figure 33. Triangular flap belt pouch, Cheyenne type, ca. 1860.
L: 31 cm, Max. W: 9.5 cm

ber of fine leather streamers dangle from the tip of the flap, and holes at the bottom corners of the pouch indicate that thongs or metal cones may have been suspended from those two points as well. Measurements are: pouch, ½″ by 4″; flap 4″ by 14″; belt (flared at ends), ½″ to ¾″ by 6′8″.

A second triangular flap belt pouch in the Derby Collection (Figure 33) is particularly handsome for its rich "pumpkin" or dark "butterscotch" background against the black designs. Other than the relatively extensive use of this unusual color, this example closely resembles the pouch collected by James Beard in design, fine workmanship, use of small seed beads, size and proportions. However, the row of beaded right triangles along outside borders of the flap is virtually identical to the motifs on the third Derby pouch, discussed below. The outer border lanes and narrow central black stripe are lazystitch. The background is "Crow stitch," the black crosses formed by a simple change of bead color within the respective rows. The outer margins of the flap are bordered with short running lazystitches of small blue pony beads. A lane of blue and white pony beads covers the pouch seams. A pair of metal cones is suspended from the upper right pouch corner. Vestiges of thongs at the other corners suggest that cones were once present at those points as well as at the tip of the flap. Stitch holes across the pouch back indicate the former existence of a belt. Measurements are: pouch, ¼″ by 3¾″; flap, 3¾″ by 12″.

The triangular flap of the third full-size belt pouch in the Derby Collection (Figure 34) is elaborated with relatively narrow lanes of lazy-stitch seed beadwork. It has a royal blue background and white-lined red isosceles and right triangles within the white border and central dividing rows. As with the other pouches in this collection, the design elements are progressively reduced in size to conform to the constricting borders. A strip of fringed leather is sewn along the margin of the flap. Metal cones containing raveled red stroud cloth are suspended by thongs through the tip of each of three points cut into the end of the flap. Beaded lanes straddle the outer edges of the pouch, covering the seams. The pouch front was pieced to obtain the desired dimensions, 3″ by 3¼″. The flap measures 3¾″ by 11″.

The fourth belt pouch in the Derby Collection (Figure 35) for a small child. The beadwork layout recalls many Northern Plains examples in that the triangular flap is divided in half lengthwise, has a decorative border, and is elaborated with a series of split diamonds (see Kurz). The seed bead colors are transparent red, light and dark blue, yellow, and white. The "Crow stitched" blue field and yellow diamonds are divided by a lane of white lazystitch beadwork. The beaded stripes at the tip of the flap recall the James Beard pouch, and are fairly common elements in that position on other examples of the genre. Two metal cones are suspended from the tip. A ⅞" German silver button attached to the face of the flap serves as a washer for tie thongs used to close the pouch. Picot edging in an unusual red-brown pony bead is worked along the outer borders of the flap and edges of the pouch, and a large lane of lazystitch beadwork decorates the outer margins of the pouch face. The attached belt consists of three lengths of leather sewn together. The bifurcated tip of one end is edged with white and the red-brown pony beads. The other forked end is edged with white and white-lined red pony beads, in addition to a few red seed beads. Measurements are: pouch, ¼" by 2⅜"; flap, 2¼" by 4¾"; belt, ¼" by 27¼".

DISCUSSION

The third Derby belt pouch in particular correlates with a number of examples the author has examined. In the Smithsonian Institution collections, number 8438 is labeled "Bullet Pouch" and was collected from the Yankton Sioux in the 1860s. The flap is decorated with seed beads applied in overlay stitch, and the white background is divided lengthwise by a row of blue diamonds. Short leather fringes outline the flap. "Sioux Scalp Pouch" number 8542 was collected at Oglalla Station, Nebraska Territory, also in the 1860s. Its seed-beaded flap is worked in rows of lazystitch—white background with black and some pink and tan. General M. M. Hazen collected belt pouch number 154026 from the Sioux. A row of diamonds divides the seed-beaded flap in the manner now familiar to us. The flap is bordered with leather fringes. Number 31032 was obtained from the Sioux by Lt. Emmet Crawford. Information from the U.S. Ordinance Bureau states, "April 26, 1875, Sioux of Dakota Territory. Pouch for Paint." Finally, number 351019 offers problematic data. "Sioux" is penned in ink in old-fashioned handwriting on the belt of this pouch. However, the collection history states, "Arapaho, Indian Territory. Gen. T. E. Wilcox, USA, gift 10-27-1930." Similar to other examples, its seed-beaded flap is divided by

Figure 34. Triangular flap belt pouch, Central Plains type, ca. 1860.
L: 31 cm, Max. W: 9.5 cm

a row of diamonds, but these diamonds are interspersed along a narrow line, such as seen on the fourth Derby pouch.

That a relatively large number of isomorphic triangular flap belt pouches with documentation exists in the Smithsonian collections is remarkable. That four, and possibly five, of these were collected from the Sioux is especially significant. Even though small repeated right triangles rather than diamonds are present on the third Derby pouch, it is evident that all these pouches are notably similar in size and proportions, beadwork techniques, and repetitive design elements. Based on comparative analysis, it may be safe to attribute numbers three and four of the Derby group to the Sioux, and even number two deserves like consideration. Certainly the general beadwork layout, techniques, motifs and color choices are comparable to known Sioux objects.

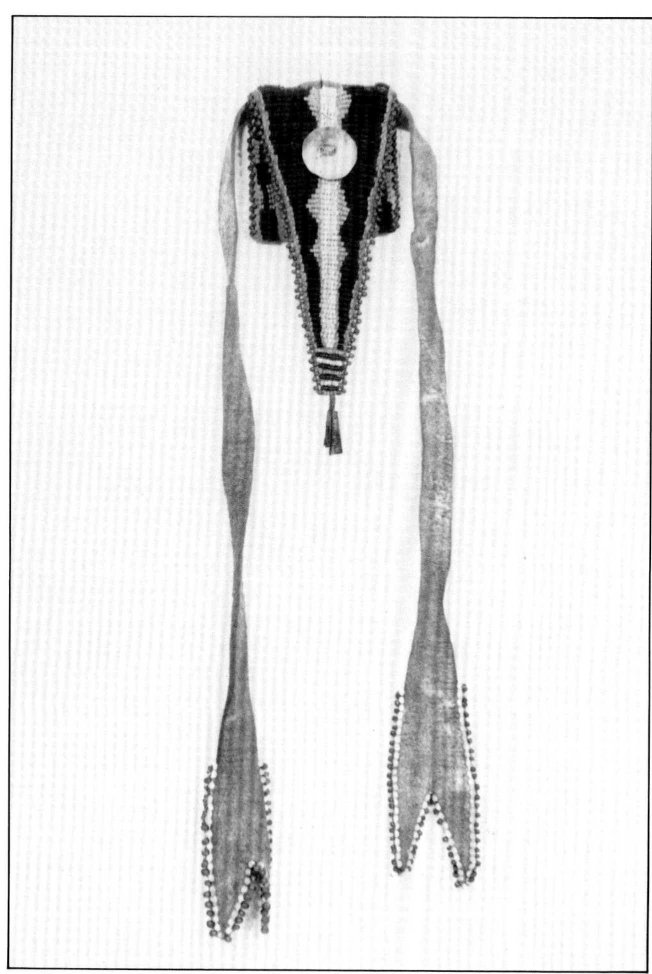

Figure 35. Child's Triangular flap belt pouch, Central Plains type, ca. 1860.
L: 13 cm, Max. W: 5.5 cm

No definite intended use or uses for belt pouches have been discovered to date, nor is there any known suggestion of gender-specificity. Indian garments traditionally did not have pockets; therefore, all manner of devices were employed to hang or carry objects on the body or clothing. Bandolier bags were worn diagonally, and various types of pouches were attached to or folded over a belt. Certain types of bandolier bags were used by Great Lakes and Prairie peoples to carry personal charms, and Plains people also carried medicine bundles on certain occasions. However, belt pouches are undoubtedly secular in nature, and a given individual could have utilized a pouch for whatever purposes he or she deemed fit. I know of one pony-beaded belt pouch that has an awl case attached to its belt, and a pony and seed-beaded example with a matching knife case attached to its belt. These recall belts with awl cases, whetstone cases, and a variety of shaped and sized pouches in sets from the Blackfoot and the Southern Plains tribes.

Collection history for a number of belt pouches has described them as conveyances for "bullets," "paint," and "scalps." None of the pouches of this genre are known to exhibit vestiges of paint, and the idea of toting scalps in belt pouches may tend to the fanciful. However, there is a correlation in actual pouch size to the so-called "strike-a-light" pouches prevalent among Plains tribes. It may be that a typical function of the triangular flap belt pouch was to store and carry fire-making equipment. A strike-a-light pouch in a modern private collection was originally purchased from a woman in Sitting Bull's band at Fort Randall, South Dakota, in 1881. The pouch was tied to the woman's belt and contained matches.

All four of the Derby triangular flap belt pouches are decorated primarily with seed beads; the child's and the one with the pumpkin background exhibit a few pony beads. This indicates that they all belong to the mid-nineteenth century. By and large the genre died out, perhaps to be largely replaced by a strike-a-light pouch type with an abbreviated flap. Although it is not known if both men and women wore triangular flap belt pouches, they would have served any number of possible uses, not only to safeguard objects, but also as beautiful accessories to clothing.

An Important Acoma Water Jar

Robert Bauver

Nestled among the clouds of New Mexico, the pueblo of Acoma has, for centuries, been an island in the flood of newcomers to the Southwest. From its mesa-top location, it has surveyed and survived the onslaught of arrows, armored conquistadors, Christianity, anthropologists, and possibly worst of all, tourists. Despite these adversities, Acoma has been able to maintain many aspects of its tradition and culture. Today, it is still much the same as it was in the past.

One—and certainly not the least—of these enduring traditions is pottery making. Acknowledged as some of the finest pottery ever produced for both its technical superiority and its artistic excellence, the pottery of Acoma has long been sought by Indian and non-Indian alike.

Historically, Pueblo pottery was primarily functional, with its decorative aspects secondary to its use. The Indian pueblos were the source of virtually all pottery in the Southwest for Indians and Spanish settlers alike. Importation of outside wares was so difficult that very few found their way into use; so few, in fact, that with only minor modifications in form to suit new cuisines, the pottery tradition remained primarily Indian in design and manufacture. Because pottery was used until it wore out or broke, only a few examples remain from the historic period, 1600-1880.

The late nineteenth century saw the advent of collectors, who sought out examples based primarily on their aesthetic qualities. This—coupled with an increased availability to the Indian of commercial cookware—was cause for a change that resulted in pottery being produced solely for its artistic merit and resale potential.

The pottery those aficionados of the last century found so appealing was made the same way it had been for hundreds of years. Like all native pottery produced in the New World, it was made entirely by hand. As in the neighboring pueblos, after the initial shape was made by coiling, it was refined by the use of various scrapers to its final form. The vessel was then coated with slip, a very fine grained clay reduced to the consistency of water. It was applied to the pot with a rag—in reddish brown to the lower portion and white to cream to the upper portion, which would serve as a background for the designs. The pigments used in decoration were black, red, and orange. Black was obtained from a boiled plant juice with a high glucose content, which would carbonize in the firing; reds and oranges were obtained from colored clays and ochres.

Figure 36. Water Jar, Acoma type, ca. 1880. (See color plate 27)

Since the clay used by Pueblo peoples was too fine-grained to support itself in the construction of anything larger than a few inches, a coarser gritty material known as temper was added to strengthen the clay body. This temper varied from pueblo to pueblo. Anything from sand to crushed stone from local outcroppings was used. The type of temper present can be the distinguishing factor in the identification of examples of pottery that appear very similar.

At Acoma, the temper used was obtained by pulverizing pottery shards. This accounts for a marked rarity of pottery fragments at the pueblo, and, as pot fragments are continually recycled, any Acoma pot intrinsically contains elements of its own history.

The Acoma water jar in the Derby Collection was "acquired from the collection of an old trader in 1891."[1] It was brought to the Northeast, where it has remained to the present date.

Because terms for dating periods of pottery development come in and out of favor among the cognoscenti, let us say this particular example typifies the Acoma water jar from the period 1880-90.[2]

There are several characteristics that justify dating this piece to within the 1880s. Assuming the collection date is accurate, the visible signs of wear allow the conclusion that this water jar saw use before its initial collection.

While this jar does not exhibit the pronounced concave flexure or under-sculpting of pots from earlier in the century, it does maintain the globular shape with the greatest diameter occurring near the midpoint. Being slightly wider than it is tall, it maintains a gentle top-to-bottom curve that would give way later in the decade to a form with a decidedly higher and more pronounced shoulder. The size and proportions are consistent with other examples from the same time period. In fact, pots of similar form can be seen being carried on the heads of two figures in a photograph by Ben Wittick of approximately 1882-85.[3]

As pottery forms evolved, so did their surface decoration. There was more of an inclination towards a balance of design and color during the 1880s. The earlier trait of a separate neck band was often omitted, leaving the entire surface as an unbroken field of decoration, as can be seen in this example. Polychromed in black and red on a white background above a reddish base, this jar exhibits a continuous, well-integrated design with all of its components working in harmonious balance.

In 1924-25, when Ruth Bunzel was performing her pioneer research on pueblo pottery, the Acoma potters stated that "the only unit or design they recognized was the jar itself." Although these comments were recorded after this jar was collected, it is safe to assume that this maxim was employed in their earlier designs.

It was also during this time that there was a strong emergence of several new design elements that the Acoma potters would incorporate into their decorative repertoire.[4] Two of these can be seen on the Derby water jar. One is the undulating band that encircles the jar, seen here as parallel red bands separated by connected, open-center, black diamonds. In other examples from this period, this band has been observed in the form of fretwork, or parallel bands of red and orange. In some cases, the gentle curves gave way to sharp angles so the band zigzags around the jar. With minor variations, the concept remains the same, where the jar is bisected into upper and lower, with the remaining spaces being filled in with similar designs. It is important to note here that where this overall design occurs on jars of this period, the elements above and below the encircling band may appear similar, but upon closer scrutiny they often have subtle, distinct differences. In later examples, these same areas are filled by identical designs.[5] In fact, the overall design this piece bears is certainly a forerunner of a design that became popular late in the nineteenth century and into the next. Numerous examples can be found in various museum collections.[6]

The other distinctive element that appears on this water jar is the hatching, or straight line fill-in. Used here in moderation, this technique would gain such favor that, within fifty years, it would become a standard method of decoration. In a 1987 article in *American Indian Art Magazine*, Richard Howard states that only two jars with documented collection dates of before 1890 show hatching in an area bordered by straight lines, while hatched leaf shape designs occur more frequently. Both of these characteristics are present on the Derby water jar. This, along with the collection date given it, would place this jar's manufacture in the very late 1880s.

Viewed now in a context alien to its origins, the Derby water jar remains a graceful blend of past traditions and evolving styles that occurred at a time of new beginnings for an age-old craft.

Color Plates

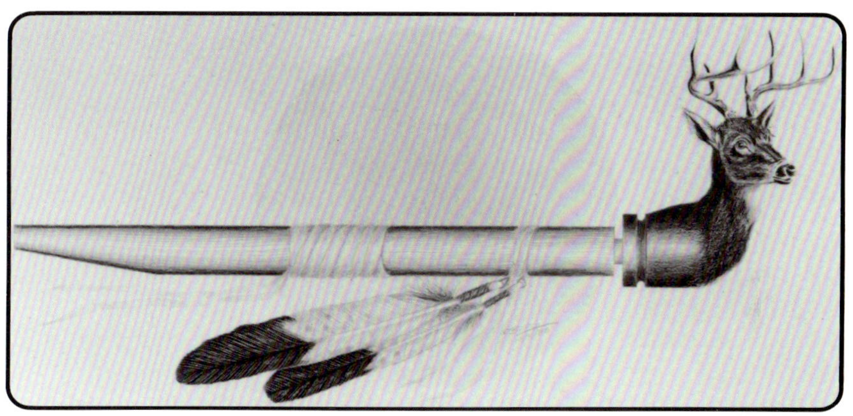

Plate 1. Shirt, Mohawk type, ca. 1840. (See essay by Ted Brasser)

Plate 2. Hat, Karuk type, ca. 1880. (See essay by Sarah Peabody Turnbaugh)

Plate 3. Quilled Box, Micmac type, ca. 1853. (See essay by Ruth Holmes Whitehead)

Plate 4. Man's Hat, Micmac type, ca. 1890. Red, green and black velvet; cotton; thread; green, yellow, lavender, red, white, clear, clam-broth, pumpkin, light and medium blue glass beads; silver metallic beads; 21 cm long, 14 cm high, 18 cm wide. For a similar example see *The Spirit Sings,* 1987, pg. 47, item 38. "Micmac man's cap made by Mary Ann Geneace, Richibucto, N.B."

Plate 5. Medicine Bag, Potawatomi type, ca. 1880. Otter skin; black trade cloth; green silk binding; red, yellow, green, lavender, pumpkin, white, clam-broth, light, medium and dark blue glass beads; brass thimbles; brass beads; 125 cm long.

Plate 6. Bandolier Bag, Santeaux type, ca. 1877. (See essay by Richard Pohrt Jr.)

Plate 7. Moccasins, Eastern Woodlands type, ca. 1850. Native tanned deerskin; silk and cotton trade cloth; white, pumpkin, grey, red and medium blue glass beads; gold metallic beads; 21 cm long, 8 cm wide.

Plate 9. Bandolier Bag, Cherokee type, ca. 1830. Dark blue wool; black silk; cotton thread; white, light blue, turquoise and pink glass beads; pouch - 19.5 cm x 19.5 cm, strap - 136 cm x 10 cm.

Plate 8. Bag, Cherokee type, ca. 1830. Dark blue wool; black silk; cotton; white, green, lavender, red, turquoise and light blue glass beads; white pony beads on edge of silk, 21 cm long, 21 cm high.

Plate 10. Moccasins, Delaware type?, ca. 1867. Native tanned deerskin; green, tan, purple and aqua silk; black, yellow, green, red, white and blue glass beads; white pony beads on edge of cuff; 21 cm long, 7.5 cm wide.
Provenance: Collection of Mary Bremmen of Lancaster, Pennsylvania. They were brought back from Ottawa, Kansas in 1867.

Plate 12. Pouch, Nez Perce type, ca. 1860. Native tanned deerskin; red, lavender, pumpkin, yellow, white, medium and dark blue glass beads; 35 cm long (including fringe), 15.5 cm wide (at top). (See essay by John Gogol)

Plate 11. Panel bag, Kaska type?, ca. 1860. Black trade cloth; cotton print; yarn; porcupine quill; white, lavender, clam-broth, red, light and medium blue, light, medium and olive green glass beads; 34 cm long, 17 cm wide. (See essay by Ted Brasser)

Plate 13. Pouch, Lipan Apache type, ca. 1850. (See essay by Jonathan Batkin)

Plate 14. Dress, Apache type, ca. 1850. (See essay by Benson L. Lanford)

Plate 15. Calumet, Eastern Sioux type, ca. 1830. Stem: wood; paint; red trade cloth; horsehair; 102 cm long. Bowl: catlinite with lead inlay; 14 cm long. (See essay by Benson L. Lanford)

Plate 16. Shirt, Lakota type, ca. 1870. (See essay by F. Dennis Lessard)

Plate 17. Doll, Apache type, ca. 1880. Native tanned deerskin painted yellow and pink; red cotton cloth; commercial leather; tin cones; cotton print fabric; brass tacks; black, blue, white and red glass beads. Extra boots. Slight damage to skirt. 44 cm. Provenance: Purchased at F. O. Bailey auction in Portland, Maine on July 1, 1982, lot 34. While I was examining this doll at the auction preview, I met the granddaughter of the woman who collected it. She told me her Grammie Bemis collected this doll on a solo trip to the southwest in 1880 and brought it back to her home in White Plains, N.Y. For similar examples see Fox and Landshoff, *The Doll,* plate 150.

Plate 18. Cape, Arapaho type, ca. 1890 (See introduction)

Plate 20. (left) Moccasins, Gros Vente type, ca. 1880. Native tanned leather; cotton cloth; white, green, red, lavender, pumpkin and dark blue glass beads. 23.5 cm long, 8.5 cm wide.
(right) Moccasins, Arapaho type, ca. 1880. Native tanned leather; rawhide; white, yellow, red and black glass beads; 24.5 cm long, 7.5 cm wide.

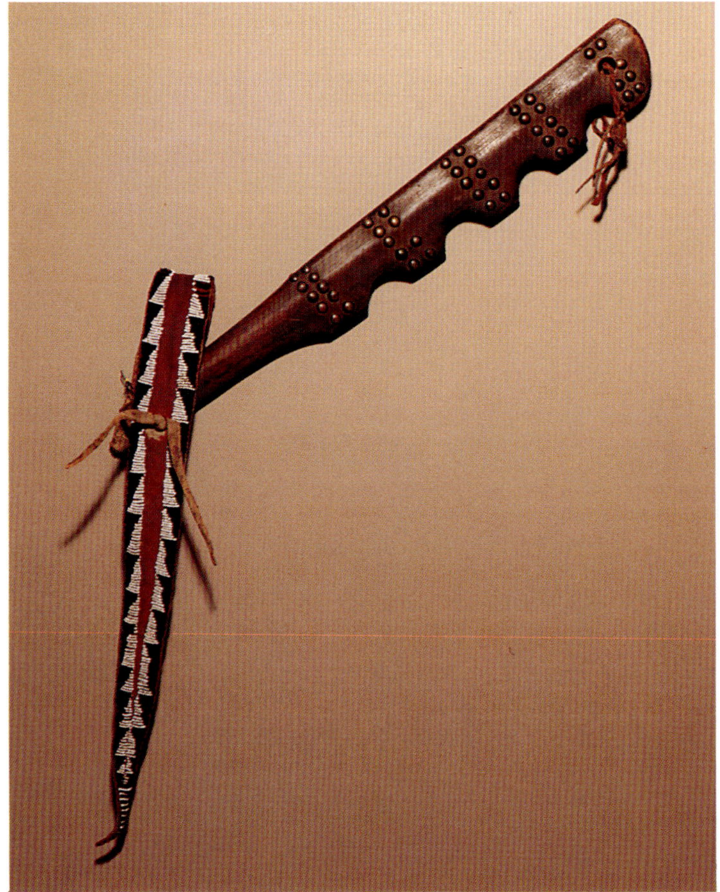

Plate 19. Pipebag, Yankton Sioux type, ca. 1860. Red trade cloth; native tanned deerskin; tin cones; procupine quill; white, black, yellow, red and green glass beads; 103 cm long, 15.5 cm wide.

Plate 21. Quirt, Lakota (Sioux) type, ca. 1860. Native tanned buffalo; red trade cloth; black and white glass beads; wood; brass tacks; commercial leather.
Handle: 45.5 cm long, 6 cm wide.
Strap: 55 cm long, 4.75 cm max. width.

Plate 22. (left to right)
Moccasins, Nez Perce type, ca. 1890. Native tanned leather stained yellow; velvet ribbon; green, white, red, clam broth, light, medium and dark blue faceted glass beads. 24 cm x 8.5 cm
Moccasins, Eastern Sioux type, ca. 1860. Native tanned leather; commercial leather sole; purple silk binding; cotton lining; lavender, green, red, pumpkin, yellow, black, medium and dark blue faceted glass beads. 28 cm x 8.5 cm
Moccasins, Koutenai type, ca. 1870. Native tanned leather; cotton binding; white, pumpkin, medium and dark blue glass beads. 25.5 cm x 8.5 cm

Plate 23. Doll, Lakota (Sioux) type, ca. 1890. Native tanned deerskin; human hair; wood; tin; 33 cm high.

Plate 24. Dolls, Lakota (Sioux) type, ca. 1870. Native tanned deerskin; red trade cloth inside tin cones; commercial leather belt; porcupine quill earrings; Male, 31 cm high; Female, 29 cm high.

Plate 25. Belt, Kiowa type, ca. 1870. Commercial leather; native tanned leather; German-silver buttons; wine red, white, medium and dark blue glass beads; trade buckles; 79 cm long, 9 cm wide. Said to be from the George Silverhorn family collection.

Plate 26. Strike-a-light, Kiowa type, ca. 1850. (See essay by David Wooley)

Plate 27. Strike-a-light, Kiowa type, ca. 1860. (See essay by David Wooley)

Plate 28. Shield and Cover, Crow type, ca. 1870. Shield: rawhide painted with red pigment. Shield cover: Native tanned buffalo hide; cobalt blue, chrome yellow, mercury vermillion and green paint; hawk feathers with trade cloth fragments; weasel stuffed with wool and decorated with faceted black glass beads as eyes and a brass trade bell in mouth; human hair wrapped with red, green and white beads at top; pouch of leather filled with an unknown substance (possibly tobacco) decorated with an animal paw which is sewn with white and lavender pony beads and dark blue and yellow glass beads. 41 cm diameter. Collected by Edward Stevens about 1890.

Plate 29. Water Jar, Acoma type, ca. 1880. (See essay by Robert Bauver)

Catalogue

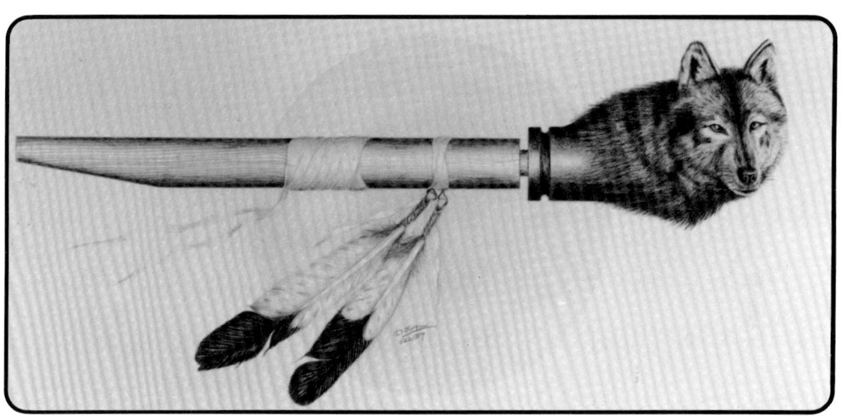

1

2

1. **Bandolier Bag**
Potawatomi type?; ca. 1890
Red trade cloth; cotton print; white, green, black, red, pumpkin and blue-grey glass beads
85 cm x 31 cm

For a similar example see Hartmann, *Die Plains — und Prärieindianer Nordamerikas* Photo number 60. Also The Hood Museum at Dartmouth College has a similar type: Churchill collection data identifies their piece as having been made by the "daughter of an Omaha Chief in Nebraska."

2. **Sash**
Menomini type; ca. 1900
Wool yarn; cotton thread; green, white, pumpkin, pink, light and dark blue glass beads
80 cm x 9 cm (not including fringe)

For a photo of a Menomini Indian wearing what appears to be this belt see Coe, *Sacred Circles,* 1976, p. 76.

3

4

3. **Bandolier Bag**
Chippewa (Ojibwe) type; ca. 1890
Black velvet; cotton print; yellow, red, dark and light green, dark and light blue, lavender and pumpkin glass beads
91 cm x 33 cm

For a similar example see Scherer, *Indians,* 1973, p. 174. Worn by One Called From A Distance, a Leech Lake Band Chippewa.

4. **Bandolier Bag**
Chippewa (Ojibwe) type; ca. 1870
Red and black trade cloth; cotton print; yellow, clear, red, green, dark and light blue, lavender and pumpkin glass beads
102 cm x 31 cm

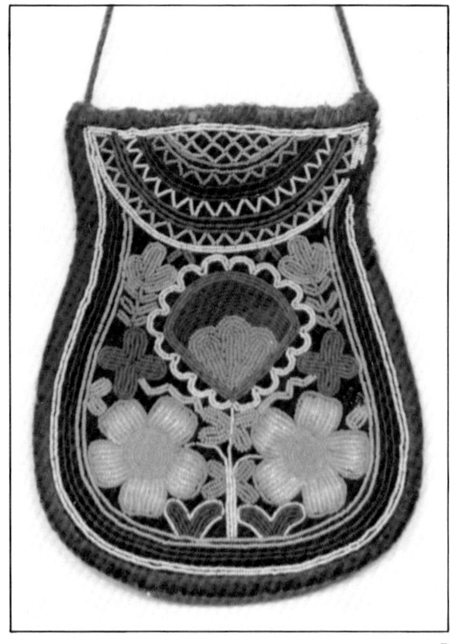

5

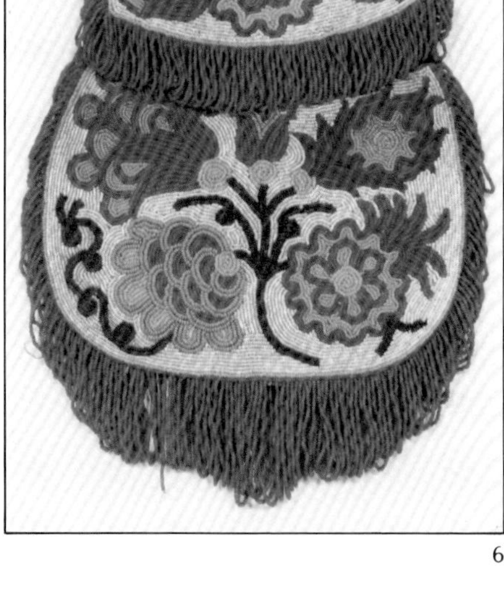

6

7

5. **Purse**
Northeast type; ca. 1880
Black velvet; cotton; silk, clear, pumpkin; white, red, yellow, lavender, green, light and dark blue glass beads
16 cm x 12 cm

For a similar example see *Handbook of North American Indians,* volume 15, 1978, p. 187. A photo shows Mercy Nonsuch Matthews, a Western Niantic, with a pouch that she made.

6. **Purse**
Chippewa (Ojibwe) type; ca. 1880
Moosehide; silk, red, yellow, green, black, light, medium and dark blue, lavender and white glass beads
28 cm x 23 cm

7. **Man's Cap, Glengarry Style**
Iroquois type; ca. 1860
Black velvet; grazed cotton; clear, white, red, green, yellow and blue glass and metal beads
L: 26 cm; W: 11 cm; H: 11.5 cm

For a similar example, see Coe, *Sacred Circles,* 1976, p. 84, item 75.

8. **Whistle**
Central Plains type; ca. 1860
Native tanned leather stained with a brown natural pigment; porcupine quills stained yellow; eagle wing bone; sinew
18 cm long (wing bone)
48 cm long (quill wrapped suspensions)

9. **Possible Bag**
Lakota (Sioux) type; ca. 1880
Native tanned buffalo hide; red trade cloth inside tin cones; canvas; green, lavender, red, light, medium and dark blue glass beads; porcupine quills
30 cm x 19 cm

10. **Ration Card or Paint Pouch**
Lakota (Sioux) type; ca. 1880
Native tanned leather; red, green, yellow, medium, and dark blue glass beads; tin cones; horsehair dyed red. Inside back of pouch is stained with Chinese vermillion
15 cm long (excluding tassels)
7.5 cm wide

8

10

9

11

11. **Moccasins**
Assiniboine type; ca. 1890
Native tanned leather with yellow and red staining; native repairs to soles; canvas uppers made from what appears to be some sort of flour or grain sack. "Toronto No. 3" is visible on outside of right moccasin; yellow, blue, black and red glass beads
24.5 cm x 8.5 cm

A tag attached to the right moccasin reads "Stony, Canada, 1929."

MOCCASINS WITH HOLES IN THE SOLES

As a child I remember hearing that some Great Lakes Indians cut a hole in the soles of their children's moccasins to thwart evil spirits.[1] This concept is not prevalent in ethnological literature, and I have never noticed any examples of these. If it is true that Great Lakes Indians did indeed cut such holes in children's moccasins, the practice may relate to five examples of Plains "two-piece, hard sole" adult moccasins that the author has examined, which have a hole purposely cut in the sole of each.

Some years ago I observed that two particular pairs of fully-beaded Sioux moccasins, circa 1890, had a diamond-shaped hole approximately one quarter or five eighths of an inch long cut through each sole at the ball of the foot, just toward center from the base of the big toe. These were the first such holes I had ever noticed, and it was immediately obvious to me that the holes were not worn spots, for the walls of each hole were still the thickness of the sole itself. I recalled the supposed Great Lakes custom, but noted that each of these pairs was for an adult male. In reflecting upon the Plains Indians' deep reverence for Mother Earth, is it possible that providing each moccasin with a small hole somehow relates to its wearer keeping in constant contact with the Earth?

I found the same treatment on a third Sioux pair of moccasins a few years later. However, in this case, each hole was round. Still later, I purchased a pair of Northern Arapaho moccasins made for an adult male that bore the same modification — a hole cut through the rawhide sole of each at the center of the ball of the foot. Again, the walls of the holes are thick, indicating that neither were these merely worn through. Each ovoid hole is about one quarter inch in length. Another pair of adult male Arapaho or Cheyenne moccasins in the Charles Derby Collection bears a similar elliptical hole cut through each sole. The happenstance of five pairs of moccasins bearing a small, purposely cut hole through the soles strongly suggests some still unknown intention on the part of the maker and/or wearer.

It has been suggested that these holes might have been made by a collector to permit hanging for display. This is undoubtedly not the case, for the location of the holes is opposite the fully-beaded vamp area of each moccasin, in the same location of each sole of the respective pairs. Anyone who has worked with rawhide knows that it is extremely tough material. It would be very difficult to cut a hole through a dry rawhide sole after a moccasin is assembled. Certainly there are other, easier ways to prepare moccasins for hanging on a wall. All these holes were cut when the rawhide was wet, before the moccasin uppers were sewn in place. In addition, the walls of the holes evidenced ground-in dirt from wear.

At this date, field work is unpromising, and so far only the single citation above has been located in the literature. However, further search may locate more examples of moccasins treated in this manner, and further study may reveal reasons for the treatment.

— Benson L. Lanford

12. **Moccasins**
Southern Arapaho or Cheyenne type; ca. 1900
Native tanned leather; rawhide soles; green, red, blue, purple and faceted gold glass beads
25.5 cm x 9 cm

Note on bottom of left moccasin reads: "Genuine Old Indian Moccasins from El Reno, Okla. Indian Reservation, from H. Wm. Selson's Private Collection."

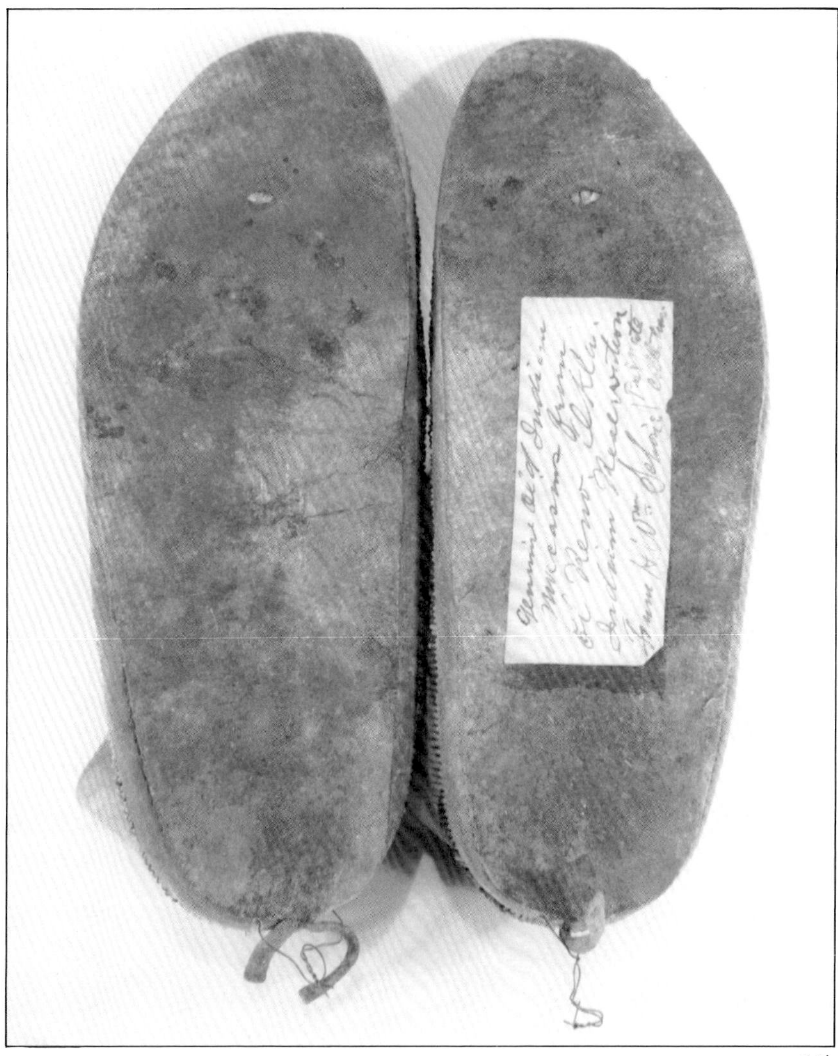

12b

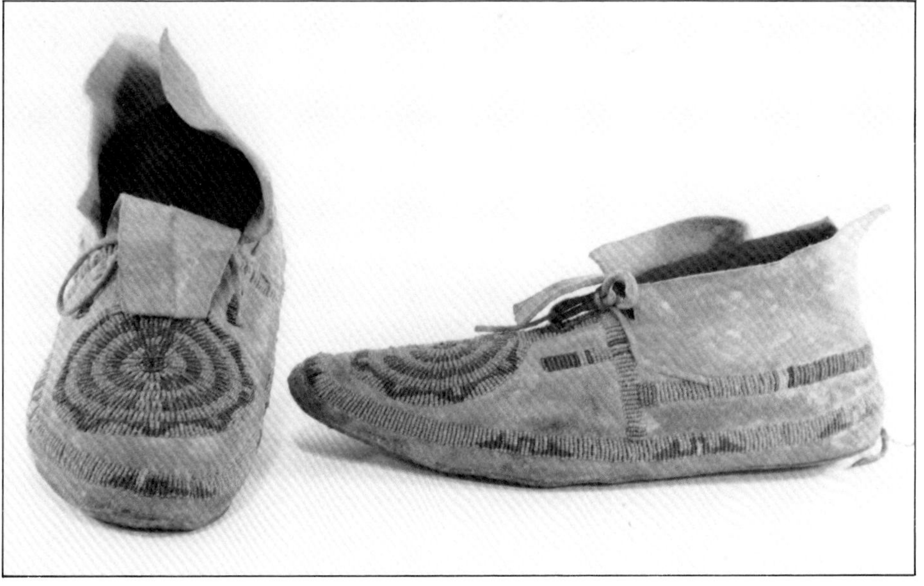

12a

13

14

13. **Moccasins**
Kiowa type; ca. 1880
Native tanned deerskin uppers stained yellow and red; rawhide soles; red trade cloth; red, white, light, medium and dark blue glass beads
25 cm x 8.5 (excluding fringe)

For a similar example see Hail, *Hau Kóla,* 1980, p. 114, no. 74.

14. **Moccasins**
Arapaho type; ca. 1890
Native tanned deerskin uppers stained yellow; cowhide (rawhide) soles; yellow, blue, medium and dark red, white, and faceted blue and green glass beads
27.5 cm x 8.5 cm

15

16

17

15. **Moccasins**
Arapaho type; ca. 1910
Native tanned deerskin uppers, stained yellow and red; cowhide (rawhide) soles; blue, red, green, faceted black and silver glass beads
27 cm x 8.5 cm

16. **Moccasins**
Nez Perce type; ca. 1890
Native tanned leather; pumpkin, lavender, green, red, yellow, white, medium and dark blue grass beads
26 cm x 9 cm

17. **Saddle Bag**
Sioux (Lakota) type; ca. 1880
Native tanned buffalo hide; red trade cloth; white, red, yellow, light and dark blue grass beads

For a similar example see Conn, *A Persistent Vision,* 1986, p. 36.

19

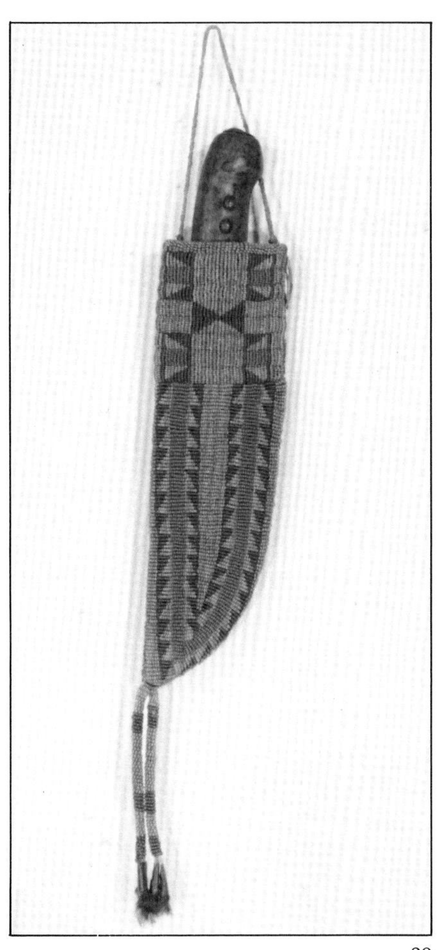

20

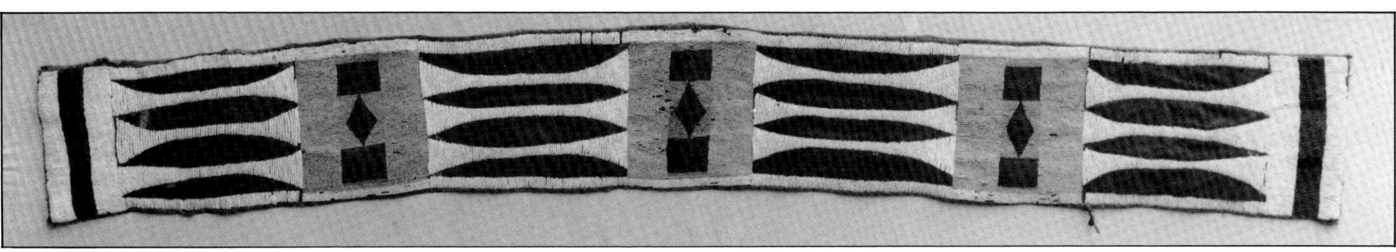

18

18. **Bandolier Strap**
Crow type; ca. 1870
Native tanned buffalo hide; cotton cloth; red, green, yellow, lavender, white, light and dark blue pony beads
154 cm long
18.5 cm wide

For a similar example see *American Indian Basketry,* no. 18, p. 22. A Wishram Indian, Martin Spedis, is wearing an old bandolier. Also *Crow Indian Art,* 1981, an essay "East Meets West: Some Observations On The Crow As The Nexus of Plateau/Upper Missouri River Art" by Gary Galante, edited by F. Dennis Lessard.

19. **Possible Bag**
Crow type; ca. 1880
Native tanned leather; red trade cloth; yellow, lavender, red, green, white, light, medium and dark blue glass beads; thread
33 cm across
20 cm high (excluding tabs)

20. **Knife Sheath**
Lakota (Sioux) type; ca. 1880
Native tanned leather; rawhide liner made from an old painted parfleche; green, red, pumpkin, medium blue glass beads; tin cones with down dyed red
38 cm long (including tassels)

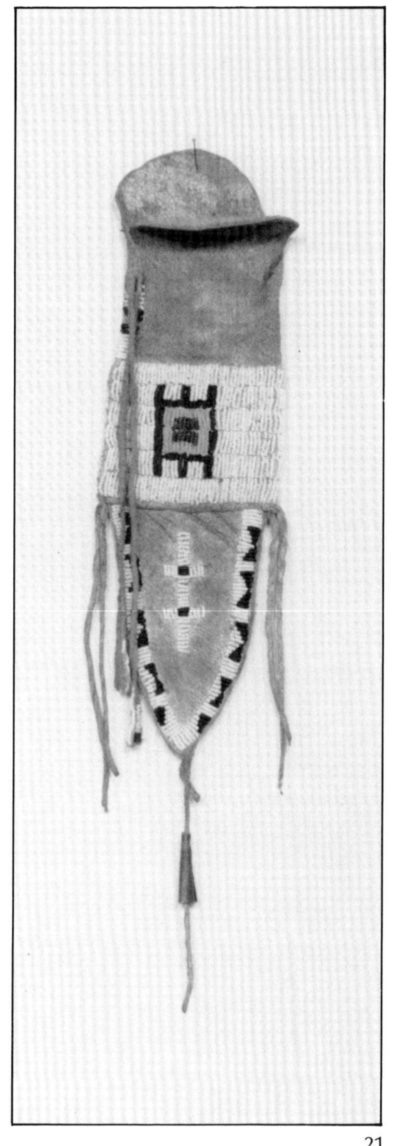

21

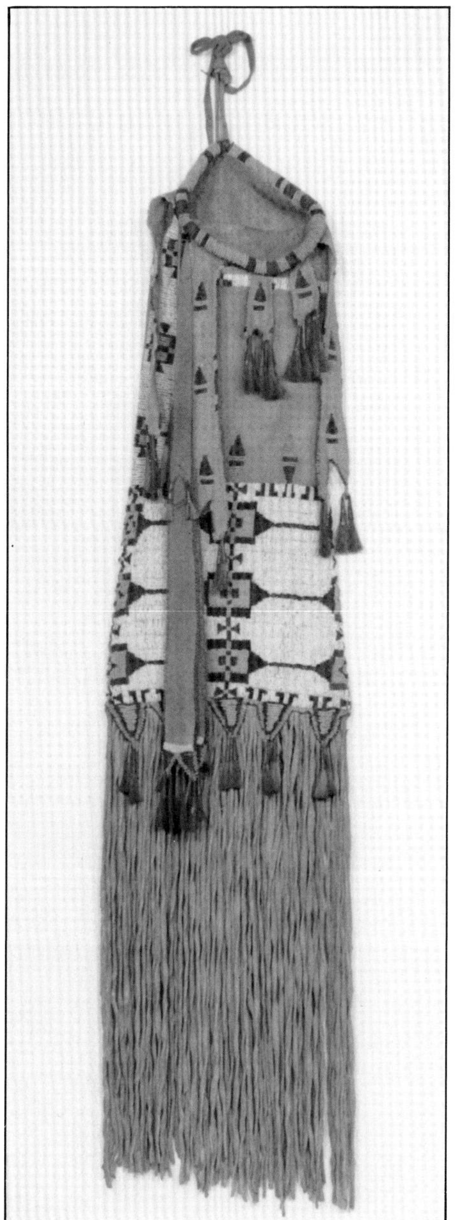

22

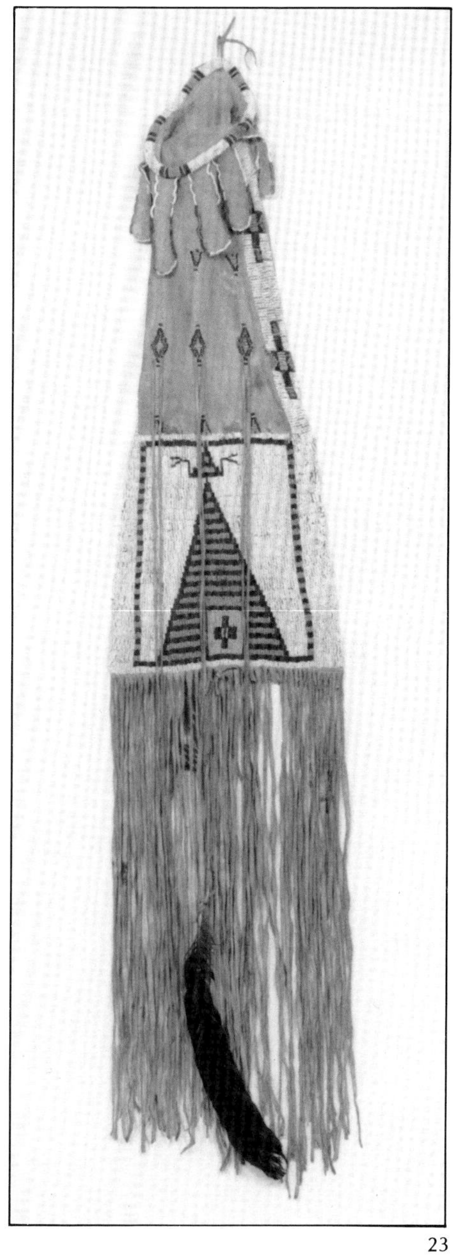

23

21. **Paint Bag**
Southern Cheyenne type; ca. 1880
Native tanned deerskin stained yellow; white, yellow, red, green, lavender and dark blue glass beads; tin cones
21 cm long (excluding drop)
6 cm wide

22. **Pipebag**
Southern Cheyenne type; ca. 1895
Native tanned deerskin stained yellow and red; green, red, yellow, white, lavender, light and medium glass beads; tin cones with red dyed horsehair
77 cm long (including fringe)
17.5 cm max. width

For similar examples see *Fred Harvey Fine Arts Collection,* 1976, p. 104, item 84 and Scherer, *Indians,* 1973, pp. 178-179.

23. **Pipebag**
Kiowa type?; ca. 1890
Native tanned deerskin stained yellow; Magpie feathers; white, red, lavender, green, yellow, light and medium blue glass beads
78 cm long (including fringe)
18 cm max. width

For a similar example see *Fred Harvey Fine Arts Collection,* p. 105, item 85.

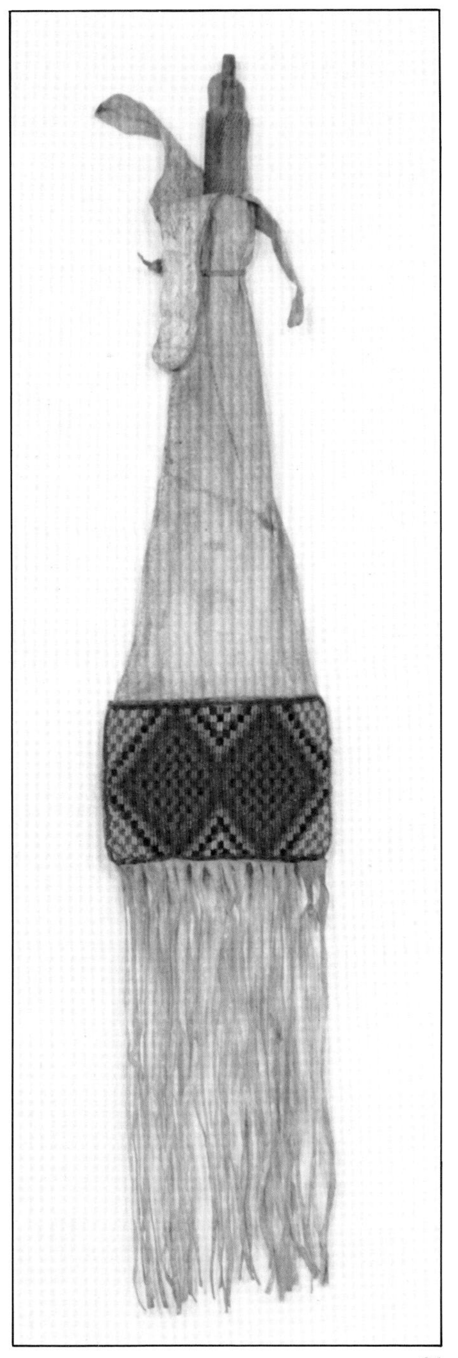

24

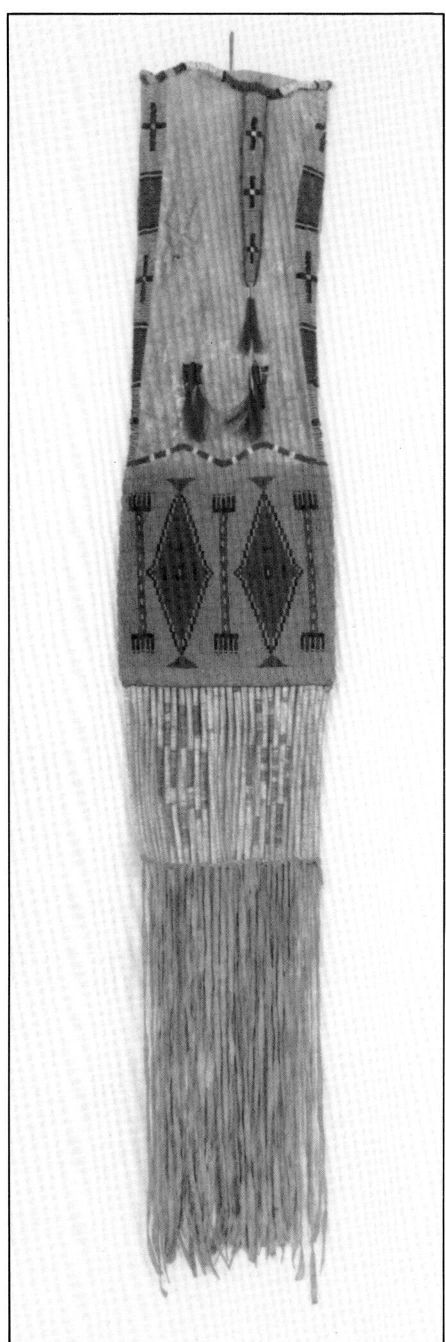

25

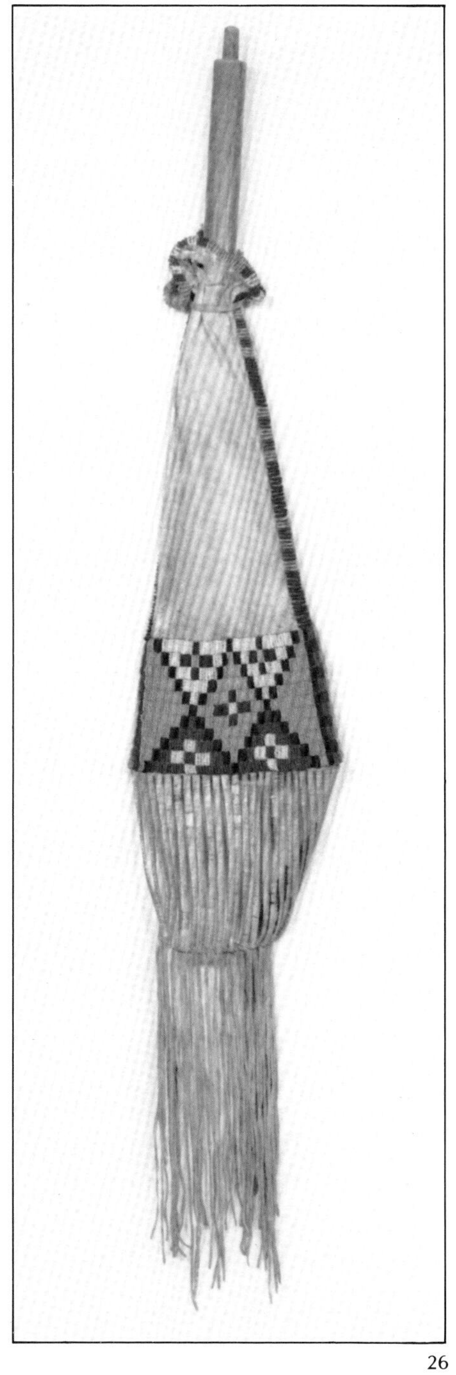

26

24. **Pipebag**
Plains Cree type; ca. 1890
Native tanned leather stained yellow; red, yellow, green, pumpkin, black, light, medium and dark blue glass beads; faceted metallic beads
70 cm long (including fringe)
15 cm max. width

For a similar example which belonged to Chief Bear see Dubin, *The History of Beads,* 1987, p. 273.

25. **Pipe Bag**
Lakota (Sioux) type; ca. 1880
Native tanned deerskin; rawhide; yellow stain; porcupine quill dyed yellow, red, white and black; red, yellow, green, white, medium and dark blue glass beads; tin cones with horse-hair dyed yellow and red
93 cm long (including fringe)
17.5 cm wide

26. **Pipebag**
Lakota (Sioux) type; ca. 1870
Native tanned deerskin; rawhide; white and yellow dyed porcupine quills; white, yellow, red, green and dark blue glass beads
80 cm long (including fringe)
17 cm max. width

28

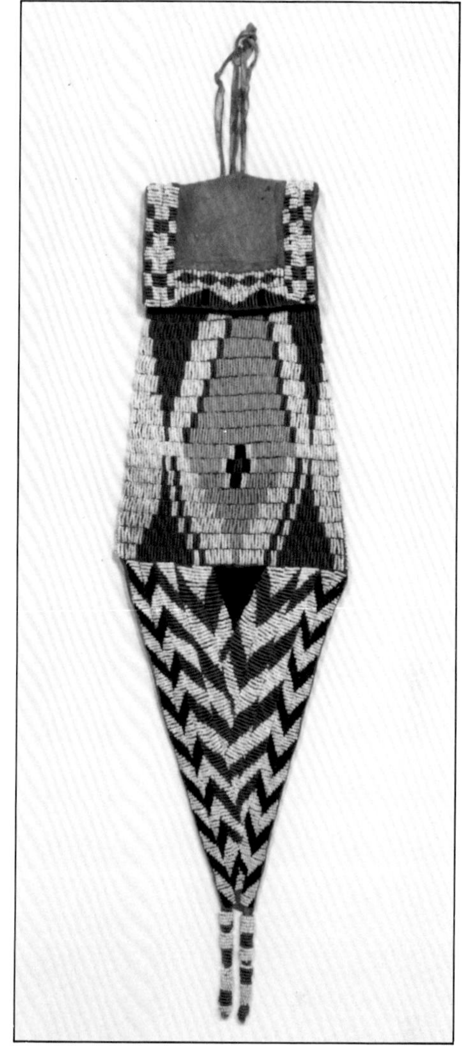

29

27

27. **Blanket Strip**
Arapaho type; ca. 1870
Native tanned buffalo hide; green, yellow, lavender, white, medium and dark blue glass beads
158 cm x 12 cm
16 cm wide at rosettes

Provenance:
Found in the attic of an estate in Marblehead, Mass.

28. **Mirror or Pipe Bag**
Ute type; ca. 1880
Native tanned deerskin; tin cones; white, yellow, black, pumpkin, green, red and medium blue glass beads
31 cm long (including tabs)
16 cm wide

For a photo of a Ute indian holding a similar type, see Pettit, *Utes, The Mountain People,* 1982, pp. 38 and 64.

29. **Pipe Bag**
Ute type; ca. 1880
Native tanned deerskin; white, red, black and light blue glass beads
59 cm long
16 cm wide (at widest point)

For a similar example see Phelps, *Arts and Artifacts,* 1976, p. 335, item number 1573.

30

31

30. **Doll**
Lakota (Sioux) type; ca. 1900
Native tanned deerskin; white, pumpkin, red, orange, lavender, yellow, light, medium and dark blue glass beads; cowrie shells; shell button; paint
35 cm high
30 cm across at arms

31. **Doll**
Lakota (Sioux) type; ca. 1890
Native tanned deerskin; white, red, yellow, green, clam-broth and dark blue glass beads; dentalia shell; cowrie shells; commercial leather; brass disks; thread; brown human hair
30 cm

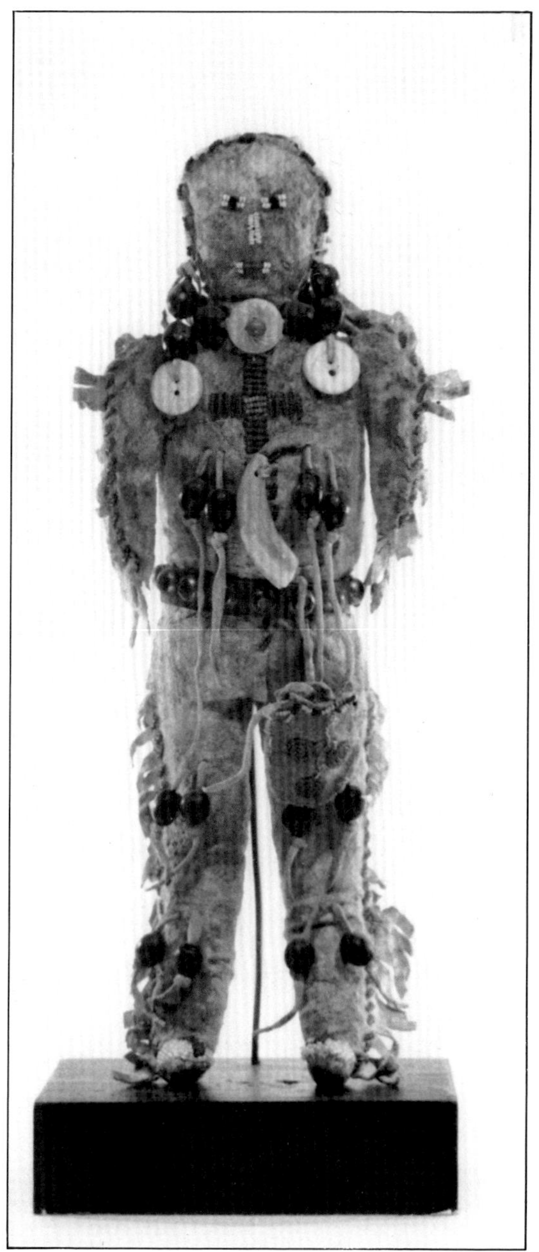

32

33

32. **Doll**
Lakota (Sioux) type; ca. 1900
Native tanned deerskin; commercial leather; mescal seeds; brass tacks; buttons; orange, red, lavender, white, clam broth, medium and dark blue glass beads; tooth
33 cm

33. **Doll**
Lakota (Sioux) type; ca. 1900
Native tanned deerskin; trade cloth; red, white, green, yellow, black, medium and dark blue glass beads; human hair
30 cm

See *American Indian Art Magazine,* vol. 14, no. 2, p. 64, Kant, "South Dakota Indian Doll Dresses." Also see Fox and Landshoff, *The Doll,* plate 147.

34

35

34. **Warbonnet Case**
Crow type; ca. 1900
Buffalo rawhide; red, green and blue earth pigments

For a similar example see Maurer, *The Native American Heritage,* 1977, p. 183, item 237.

35. **Necklace**
Sioux (Lakota) type; ca. 1870
Commercial leather; deer hooves; red paint; metal and glass watch part
87 cm

For a similar example see Maurer, *The Native American Heritage,* 1977, p. 156, item 185. Also see Brown and Felton, *The Frontier Years,* 1955, pg. 20, for a photo of "Snake Whistle, a young Cheyenne warrior, 1879." One of these necklaces is draped across his leg.

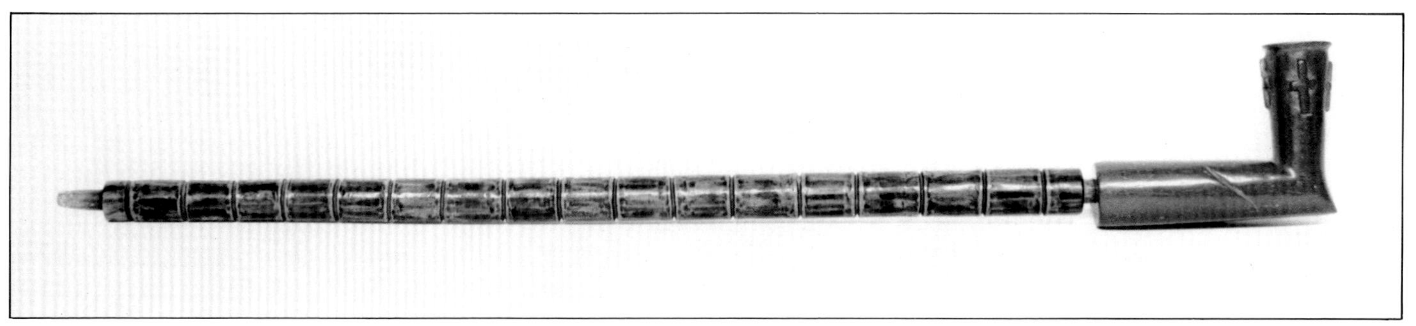

36

36. **Pipe**
Pawnee type; ca. 1860
Wood, catlinite
Stem L: 52 cm
Bowl L: 11.2 cm; W: 3.2 cm; H: 8.2 cm

The unique sacred bundle system of the Skidi Pawnee is the basis of their social and political organization. There were several types of bundles used by the Pawnee. Village bundles were divided into two groups: those deriving their powers from the star spirits and those having powers from animals. Star spirit bundles control only food supply and war; while animal power bundles control health and disease. Personal warrior bundles were considered part of Village bundles or the more important Society bundles. The functions of a Society bundle varied. There were two exclusively for hunting, six for war, and two for either. Sacred bundles were called chuharipiru (chuhuru, rainstorm; ripiru, wrapped up). The powers of the bundles come from the West, home of the thunderers who are responsible for the rainstorms. When the first thunder is heard in the spring the keeper of each bundle must immediately open it with the proper procedure and make an offering of dried buffalo meat to the powers in the West. After this and when the grass began to grow, all societies held ceremonies for the renewing of lances. It was at such a ceremony described by James Murie in *Pawnee Indian Societies* that a pipe much like the Derby example was used.

"Known-the-leader said: . . . Knife-chief will now rise and take the pipe I have filled." Murie then went on to say, "Knife-chief rose and took the pipe which belongs in a sacred bundle. It is very old. The bowl is large; the stem smooth and round and represents the windpipe through which the prayers of the people pass." The pipe is illustrated on pg. 566, fig. 5: "Pipe for the Two Lance Society. The bowl is of red stone, the stem round, marked with black bands to represent a trachea, which it symbolizes."

John Ewers in *Plains Indian Sculpture,* pg. 132, fig. 119, illustrates another similar example. The caption reads: "Sacred pipe of peace and war; Pawnee, collected by George A. Dorsey, 1900; catlinite, wood stem." Catalogue information at the Field Museum notes that there is no stem with the pipe bowl (personal communication with Janice B. Klein, registrar). However, the bowl is strikingly similar to the Derby example. There are two mammals, a man, a woman and a turtle carved in relief on the Field Museum example whereas there are four crosses carved in relief on the Derby example. —C.D.

37. **Tobacco Pouch**
Ute type; ca. 1860
Native tanned leather; blue, white and yellow glass beads
18.5 cm long (including tabs)
6.5 cm wide

See O. O. Howard, *My Life and Experiences Amoung Our Hostile Indians,* 1907, p. 411 for a photo of a Ute Indian from 1868 wearing a similar pouch. Years ago I saw a pony-beaded pouch like this one for sale in the southwest. Note the similarity of form to Navajo tobacco canteens.

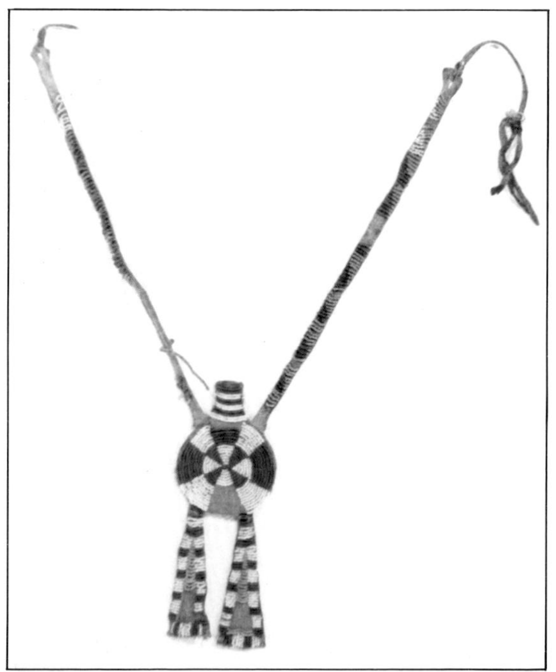

37

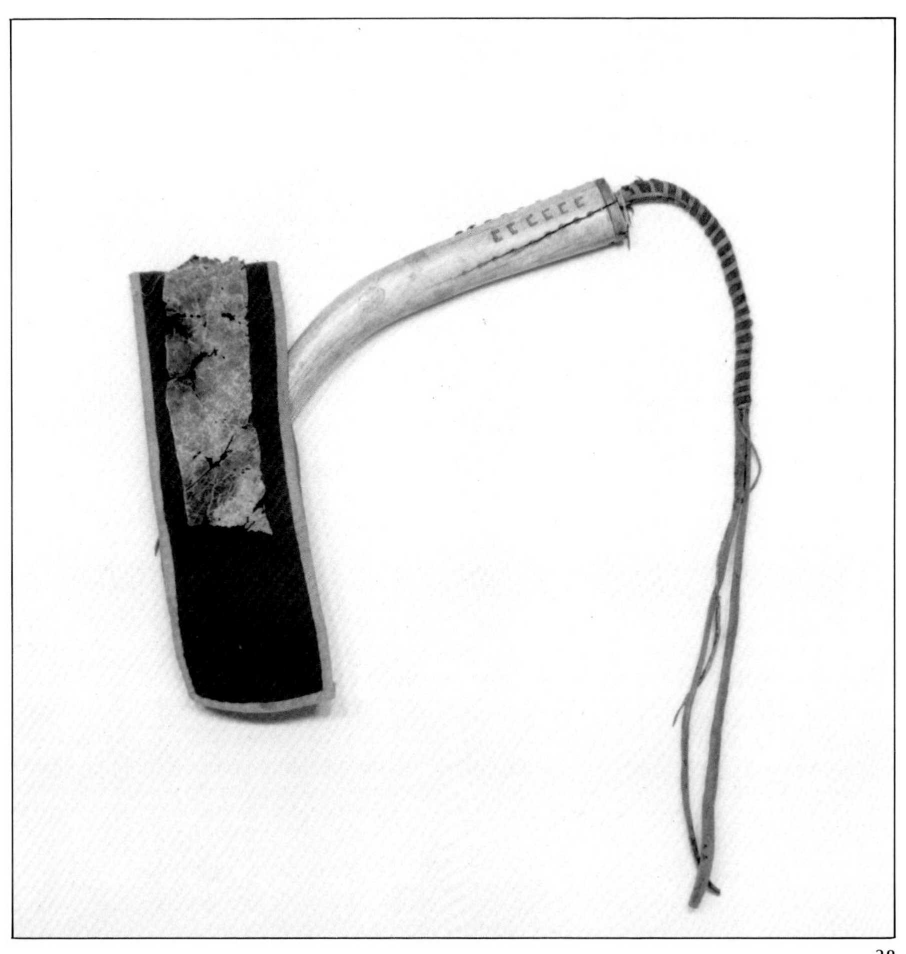

38

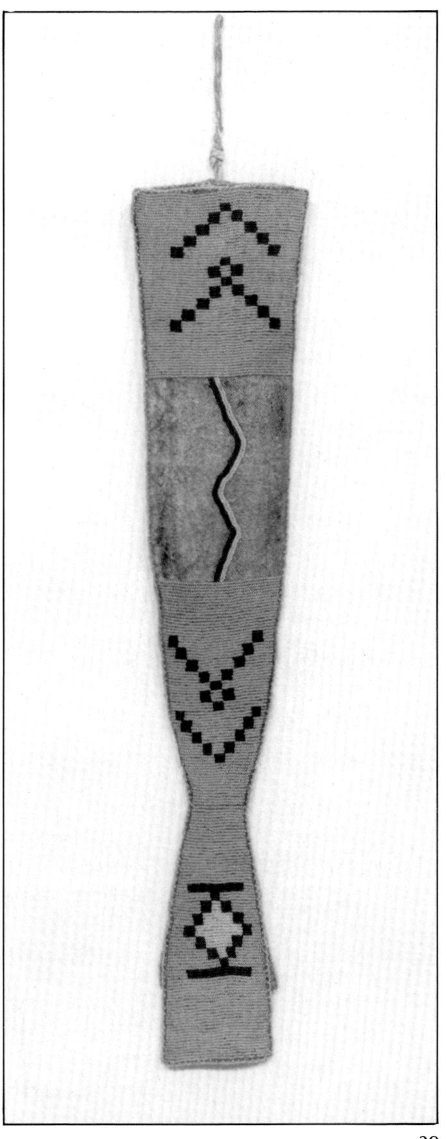

39

38. **Quirt**
Northern Plains type; ca. 1870
Elk antler; Native tanned buffalo hide sewn with thread onto red trade cloth; cotton edging on strap; rawhide covered with red trade cloth and wrapped with native hide stained green; brass tacks. Old label attached; wood plug
Elk handle - 35 cm long

Provenance:

Puchased at a Boston, Mass. antique jewelry store. I had about an hour to kill one summer afternoon in Boston. I ventured down an alley and discovered a tiny antique jewelry store that seemed like a possible spot to find an old piece of Indian jewelry. I was buzzed in to find that they only had a couple of modern Indian pieces. As I was on my way out, I turned around and said to the owner, "What I'm really looking for are Indian Artifacts." He stopped me and pulled a black velvet jewelry tray out from under a counter. I couldn't believe it — there was the Elk Antler Quirt I had dreamed of for many years. The owner told me that the piece had just been left on consignment by a local family. They had recently removed it from a museum where it had been on loan for over twenty years. I was able to purchase the piece. I still smile at the memory of this encounter; it was one of those times when I was at the right place at the right time.

39. **Knife Sheath**
Blackfeet type; ca. 1890
Native tanned leather; thread; lavender, yellow, medium and dark blue glass beads
59.5 cm long

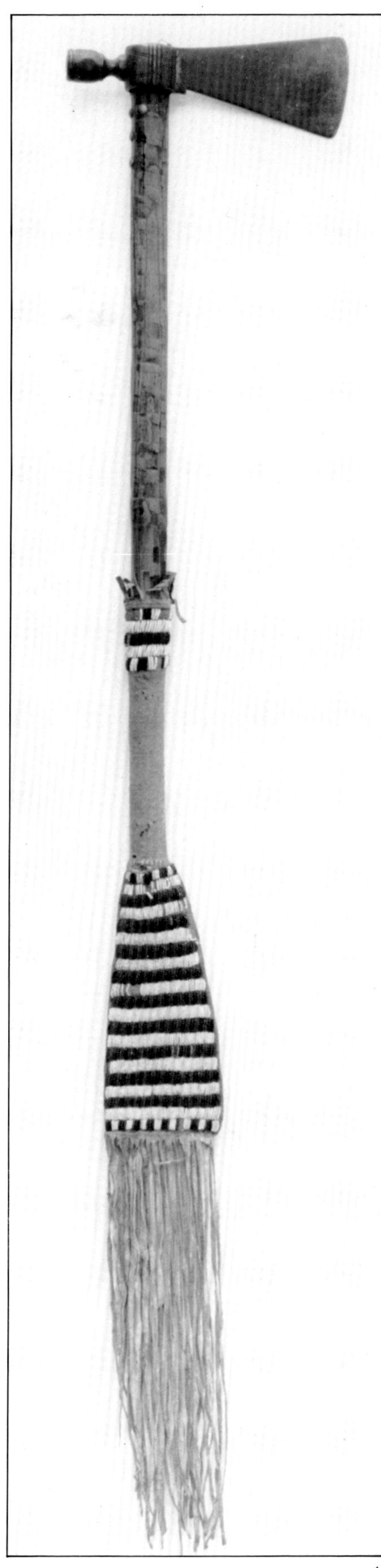

40

41

40. **Pipe Tomahawk**
Central Plains type; ca. 1860
Iron blade, haft with brass tacks at blade end and file branding on upper two-thirds; buffalo sleeve at handle end is decorated with black and white glass beads
58.5 cm long (excluding drop)
Blade 20.5 cm long
Drop 68 cm long (including fringe)

Provenance:
Arnold Chernoff collection. See Peterson, *American Indian Tomahawks,* 1971, item no. 46 and no. 49 for other examples with similar drops.

41. **Mirror Bag**
Arapho type; ca. 1900
Commercial leather; Native tanned twisted fringe; tin cones; German silver button; white, black, lavender, aqua, red-orange, and dark blue glass beads
47 cm x 17 cm

For similar types see Kroeber, *The Arapaho,* 1983, p. 96. The rosette on the center of the flap is in a style frequently used by the Kiowa-Comanche. Also see Koln, *Indianer Nordamerikas,* 1979, back plate no. 78.

42

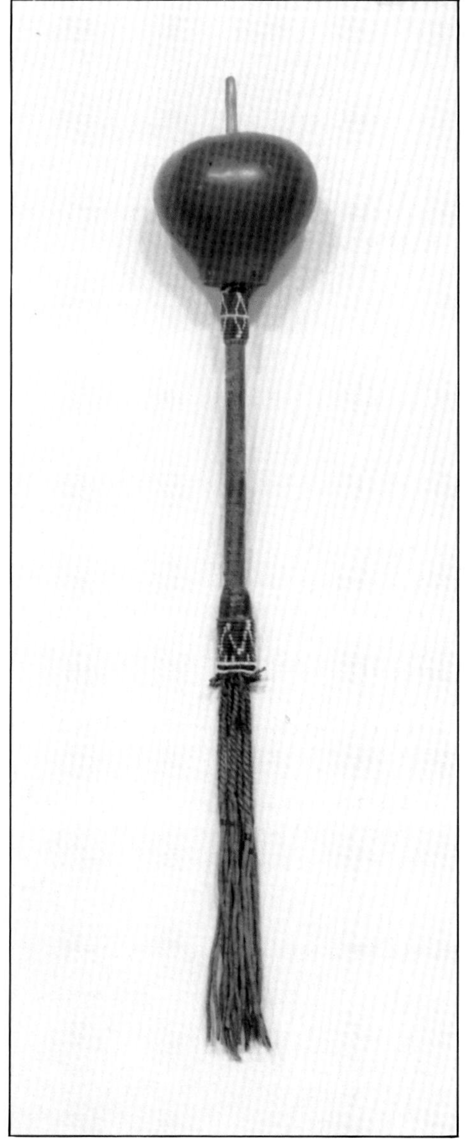

43

42. **Fan** (possibly used in Peyote Ceremony)
Southern Plains type; ca. 1890
Native tanned deerskin; brass tacks; golden eagle feathers; eagle down dyed red; red, white, black, green, medium blue, orange, faceted silver glass beads
65 cm long (including fringe)

For a similar type see Powers, *Indians Of The Southern Plains,* 1971, pp. 30, 99. Also see Capps, *The Old West: The Great Chiefs,* 1975, p. 129.

43. **Peyote Rattle**
Kiowa type; ca. 1890
Native tanned leather stained yellow; German silver hand-made beads on fringe; wood; gourd; nails; twine; dark red, white, medium and dark blue faceted glass beads
43 cm long (including fringe)

44. **Strike-A-Light and Awl Case**
Kiowa type; ca. 1880
Commercial leather; Native tanned leather; tin cones; shell hair pipes; red, green, white, lavender, yellow, light, medium and dark blue glass beads; several large glass trade beads
Strike-A-Lite: 15 cm long (from top of flap to bottom of tin cones)
8 cm max. width
Awl case: 21 cm (from top of case to bottom of tin cones)
2.5 cm max. width

For a similar example see Hail, *Hau Kóla,* 1980, p. 201, item no. 261, no. 262.

45. **Whetstone Case**
Kiowa type; ca. 1880
Commercial leather; native tanned leather; tin cones; brass brads; red, white, yellow, light and dark blue glass beads
14 cm long (excluding twisted fringe)
4 cm wide

For a similar example see Belous and Weinstein, *Will Soule,* 1969, p. 105.

46. **Child's Belt**
Kiowa-Comanche type; ca. 1880
Commercial leather; iron buckle; tin cones; German silver conchos; brass bell; brass beads; yellow, red, green, black, white, light, medium and dark blue glass beads
56 cm

For a similar example see *American Indian Art Magazine,* vol. 3, no. 4, p. 71, McGreevy, "The Dyer Collection at the Kansas City Museum."

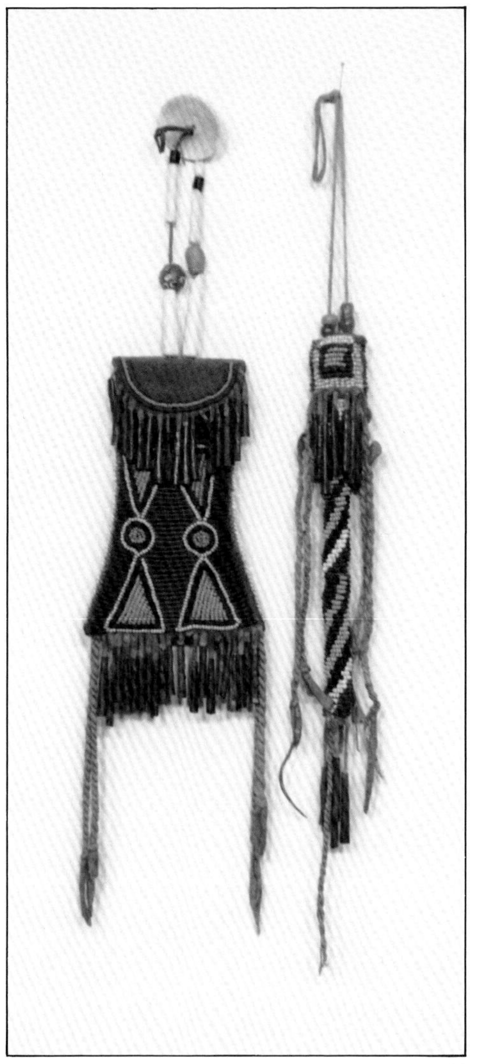

44

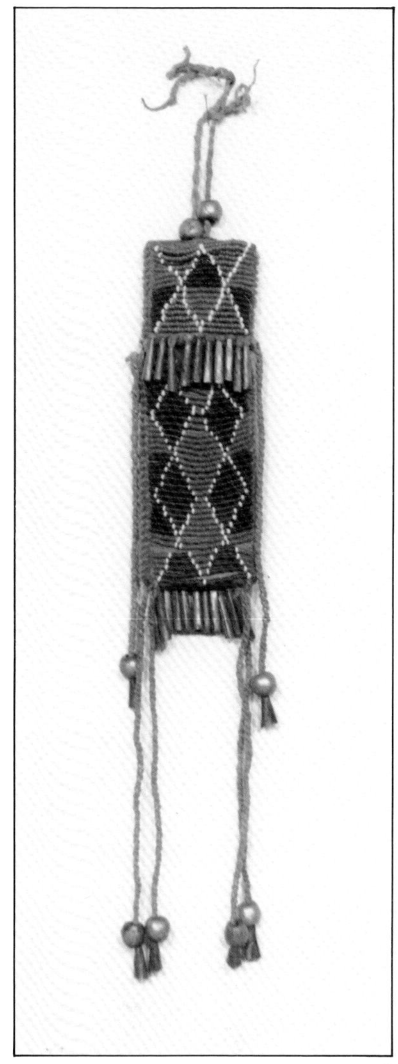

45

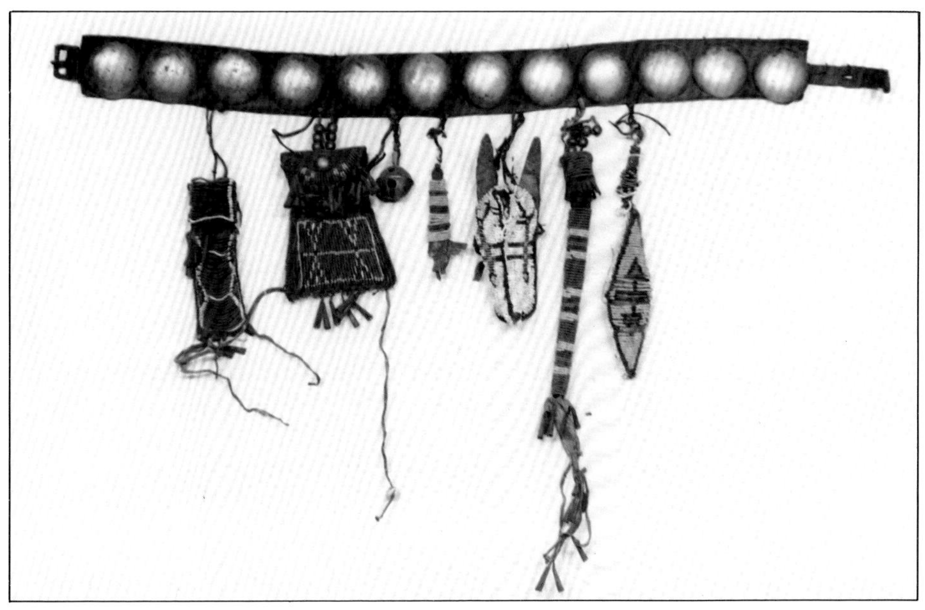

46

47

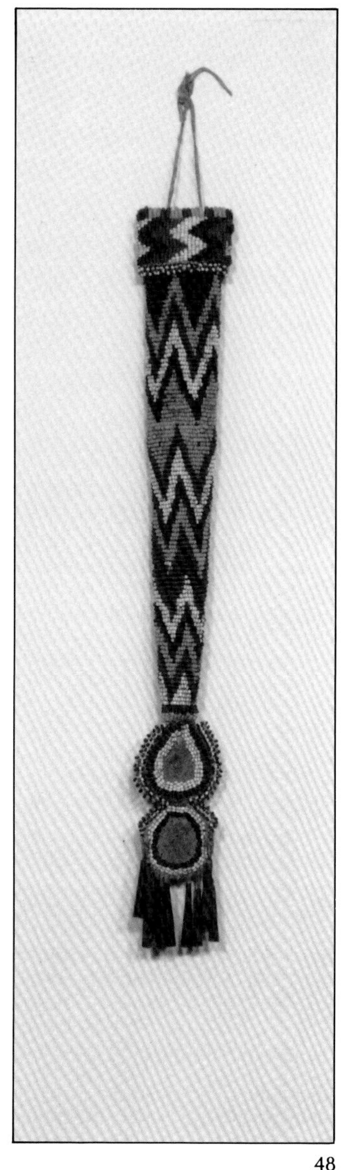
48

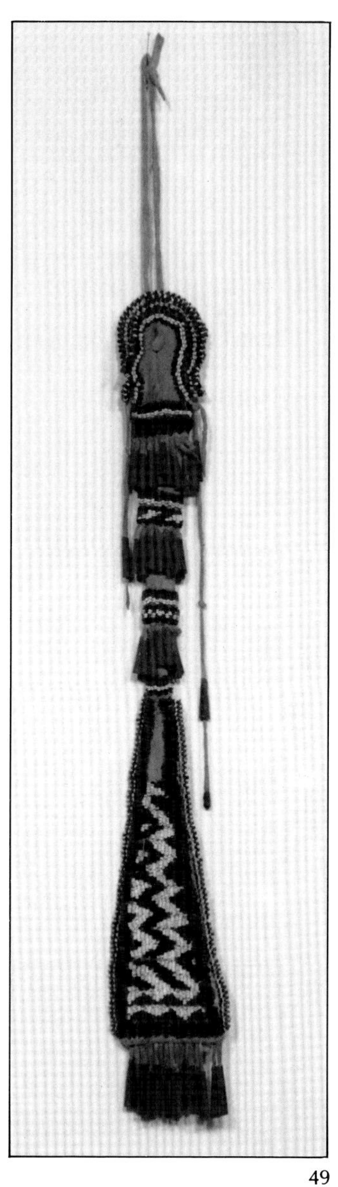
49

47. **Pouch**
Apache type; ca. 1900
Native tanned deerskin; tin cones; white, green, red and lavender glass beads; Navajo silver button
15 cm long (including tin cones)

48. **Awl Case**
Apache type; ca. 1890
Native tanned deerskin (stained yellow); yellow, white, green, red and dark blue glass beads; tin cones
34 cm long (including tin cones)

For other Apache awl cases see Ferg, *Western Apache Material Culture,* 1987, color photo 9.

49. **Awl Case**
Apache type; ca. 1880
Native tanned deerskin; black, white and red glass beads; tin cones
44 cm long (including tin cones)

50. **Pouch**
Apache type; ca. 1890
Native tanned deerskin; green, lavender, black, white, red, yellow and medium blue glass beads; thread. Pouch is lined with an unknown material and what appears to be pitch.

51. **Basketry Tray**
Apache, ca. 1930
Willow; devil's claw
27.5 cm diameter
7 stitches per cm

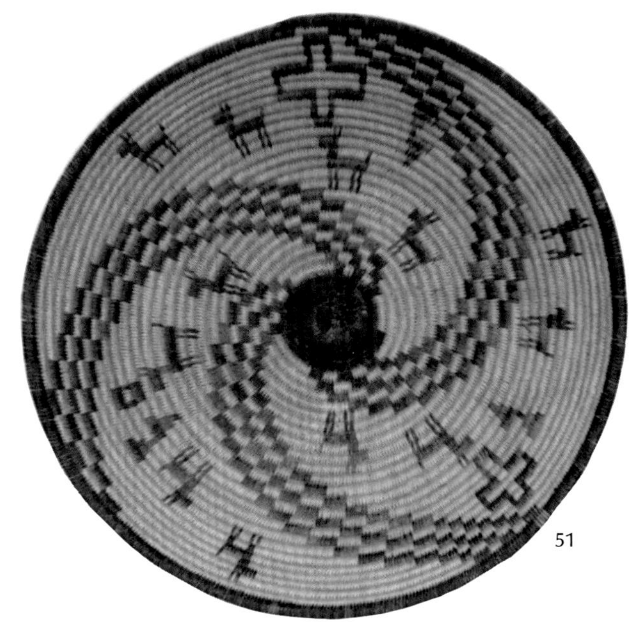
51

52. **Moccasins**
Apache type; ca. 1860
Native tanned deerskin stained orange; rawhide soles; white, medium and dark blue glass pony beads
25 cm x 9 cm

53. **Moccasins**
Apache type; ca. 1880
Native tanned deerskin stained yellow; rawhide soles; black, red, white and lavender glass beads
23 cm x 7.5 cm

52

50

53

54

56

55

54. **Pouch**
Apache type; ca. 1890
Native tanned deerskin (part stained yellow); tin cones; white, red, pumpkin, black, light and medium blue glass beads; clear and dark blue large glass beads
9 cm long (excluding tin cones)

For a photo of an Apache man wearing a similar pouch see *American Indian Art Magazine,* vol. 6, no. 3, p. 30, Ferg, "Apache Fiddle Maker."

55. **Medicine Pouch**
Apache type; ca. 1880
Native tanned deerskin; black, red, green and yellow paints
30 cm long (including fringe)

For a similar example see Howard, *My Life and Experiences Amoung Our Hostile Indians,* 1907, p. 47, plate 1.

56. **Medicine Pouch**
Apache type; ca. 1890
Native tanned deerskin; red and black paint
42 cm long (including fringe)

57

58

57. **Basketry Tray**
Yavapai Apache type; ca. 1900
Willow, devil's claw
27 cm diameter
7 stitches per cm

58. **Storage Jar (Olla)**
Yavapai Apache type; ca. 1900
Willow; devil's claw
36.5 cm high
32 cm max. width

59

61

62

60

59. **Basketry Tray**
Pima type; ca. 1930
Willow, devil's claw, grasses or cattail stems
35 cm diameter
8 stitches per cm

60. **Basketry Tray**
Pima type; ca. 1900
Willow; devil's claw; grasses or cattail stems
46 cm diameter
4 stitches per cm

63

61. **Basketry Tray**
Pima type; ca. 1930
Willow; devil's claw; grasses or cattail stems; blue glass bead
13 cm diameter
5 stitches per cm

62. **Basketry Tray**
Pima type; ca. 1920
Willow; devil's claw; grasses or cattail stems
14.5 cm diameter
7 stitches per cm

63. **Pictorial Rug**
Navajo type; ca. 1910
Handspun wool; red, orange, green, brown, grey, black and white native vegetal and aniline dyes
178 cm x 156 cm

For a weaving probably by the same hand, see cover photo in George Wharton James, *Indian Blankets and Their Makers,* Dover Edition, 1974. About this weaver, James says: "She is one of the inventive geniuses in design, whose taste invariably goes to figures. Horses, sheep, cattle, men, women, etc., she loves to picture as she weaves, and her skill in manipulating the yarn is as great as her designing ability."

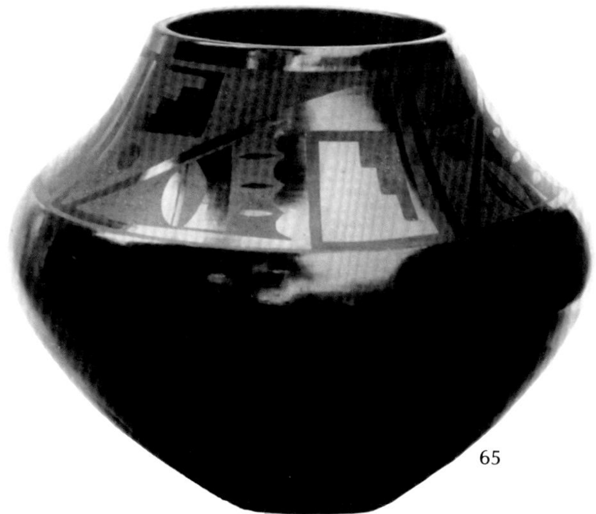

65

66

64

64. **Polychrome Jar**
Acoma Pueblo; ca. 1890
Clay; white, black, light orange and dark orange mineral paints
29.5 cm max. width
31.5 cm high

Provenance:

Purchased from a Vermont antique dealer at a Massachusetts outdoor antique show. A week earlier this dealer had purchased the pot at a cabin in the Adirondacks which was only accessible by canoe. On the return trip the pot fell against the side of the canoe. A small chip was broken from the rim and lost in the water.

67

68

65. **Black on Black Jar**
Tonita and Juan Roybal
San Ildefonso Pueblo; ca. 1920-30
Clay; black mineral and vegetal paint
30 cm max. width
28 cm high
Signed "Tonita"

66. **Polychrome Jar**
Zia Pueblo; ca. 1890
Clay; orange, white and black mineral paints
31 cm max. width
26 cm high

67. **Black and White Jar**
Acoma Pueblo; ca. 1900
Clay; orange, black and white mineral paints
29 cm max. width
28 cm high

68. **Rug**
Navajo type, Two Grey Hills style; ca. 1930
Dark brown, light brown, beige and white natural vegetal dyes
125 cm x 187 cm

69

71

69. **Candle Stick**
Hopi Pueblo; ca. 1920
Clay; red and black mineral paint
10 cm high

71. **Rug**
Navajo type; ca. 1920
Handspun wool; grey, brown, orange, red and white natural vegetal and aniline dyes
100 cm x 57 cm

72. **Pictorial Rug**
Navajo type; ca. 1930
Handspun wool; red, green, orange, yellow, blue, brown, black and white natural vegetal and aniline dyes
87 cm x 138 cm

70. **Polychrome Jar**
Zuni Pueblo; ca. 1890
Clay; orange, black and white mineral paints
31 cm max. width
25 cm high

For a similar example see Frank and Harlow, *Historic Pottery of the Pueblo Indians;* 1974; p. 146, item 155.

70

72

73

73. **Polychrome Jar**
Hopi Pueblo; ca. 1920
Clay, orange, black and cream mineral paints
33.5 cm max. width
18 cm high

Provenance:

Purchased from a Vermont private collector. This jar was collected from the Nampeyo house in 1920. There was a snapshot taken of Nampeyo in the doorway of her home the day this pot was purchased from her. There were also some blue corn tortillas that were given to the collector by Nampeyo. There are two inscriptions on the bottom: "Nampeyo — old type and Nampeyo's daughters pottery (old type)." Several experts of Southwestern pottery who have seen this pot agree that it was molded by Nampeyo and painted by one of her daughters.

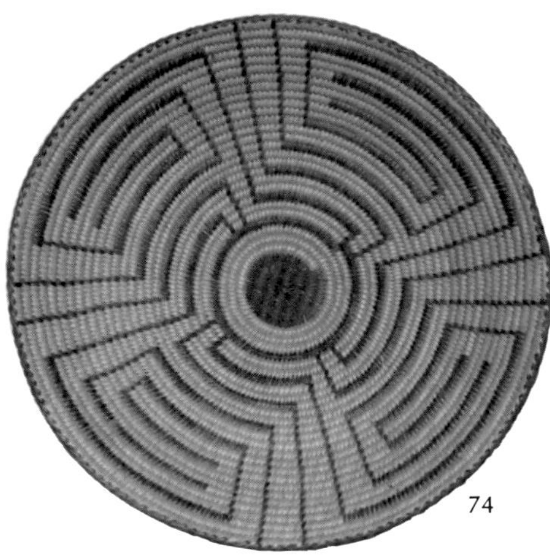
74

74. **Basketry Tray**
Pima type; ca. 1920
Willow; devil's claw; grasses or cattail stems
22 cm diameter
6 stitches per cm

75. **Germantown Blanket**
Navajo type; ca. 1880-1890
Four-ply commercial synthetic-dyed red, black, green, purple and brown wool yarn
86 cm wide
128 cm long (including fringe)

76. **Figure**
Tesuque Pueblo; ca. 1880
Clay containing mica; yellow and green paint over a cream slip
35 cm high

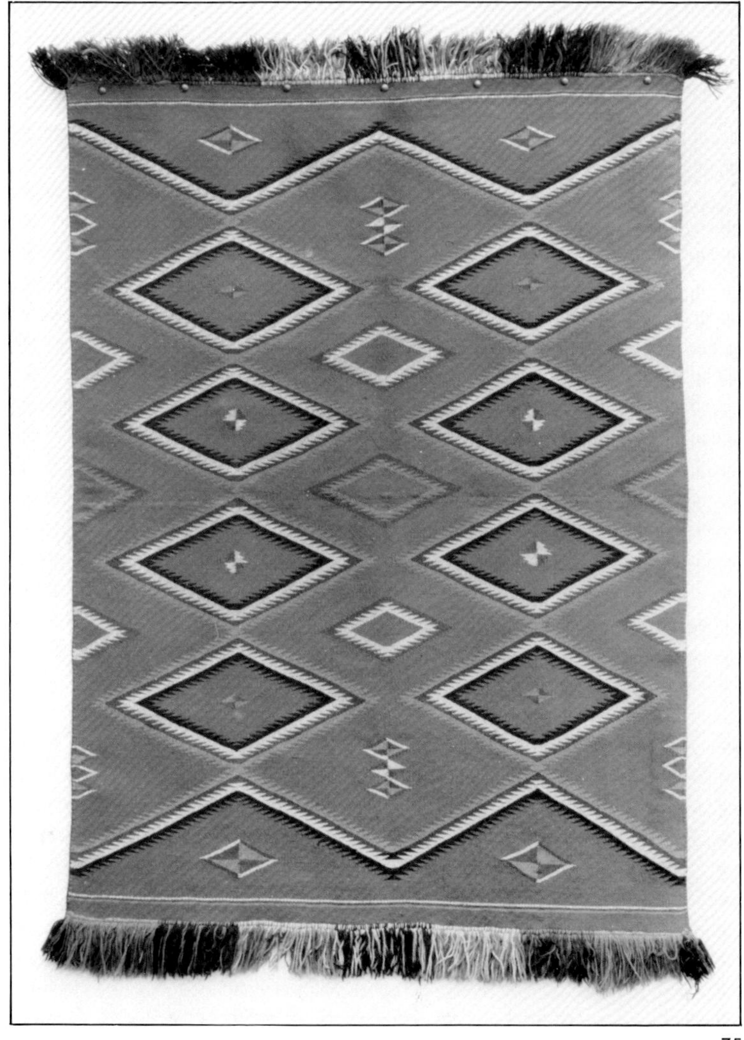
75

76

77. **Basketry Bowl**
Washoe *Degikup*
Willow and bracken fern on a 3-rod foundation; flicker feathers
11.4 cm high
14.4 cm diameter at top

Probably the work of "Minnie Dick, a full blooded Paiute who married a Washoe man (Washoe Dick) and combined elements of Paiute technique with Washoe decorative style in her weaving. Her work was always considered Washoe by Cohn." (Personal communication with Marvin Cohodas)

77

78. **Basketry Bowl**
Maidu type; ca. 1880
Sedge and redbud on a three rod foundation
16 cm high
30 cm max. diameter
6-7 stitches per cm

78

79. **Basket**
Chemehuevi type; ca. 1914
Willow; devil's claw
15.5 cm high
19 cm max. width

Provenance:
Purchased along with several other Chemehuevi baskets from a New York antique dealer. He acquired them from a man who brought them back from Needles, Ca. in 1914.

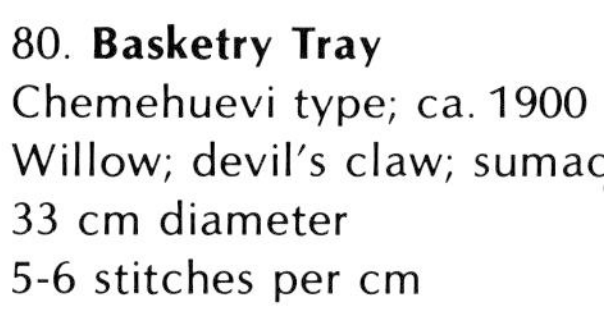

79

80. **Basketry Tray**
Chemehuevi type; ca. 1900
Willow; devil's claw; sumac
33 cm diameter
5-6 stitches per cm

80

81. **Basketry Tray**
Chemehuevi type?; ca. 1930
Willow; devil's claw
18.5 cm diameter
7 stitches per cm

82. **Cooking Bowl**
Maidu type; ca. 1890
Willow and redbud on a three-rod foundation
39 cm high
58 cm max. diameter
4 stitches per cm

81

82

83. **Basketry Bowl**
Mono Lake Paiute type; ca. 1900
Sedge root?; devil's claw and redbud on a 3-rod foundation
Rim is finished in a "whip-stitch"
7.5 cm high
14.5 cm max. diameter
10 stitches per cm

"Appears to be the work of Carrie Bethel." (Personal communication with Marvin Cohodas)

84. **Basketry Bowl**
Cahuilla type; ca. 1920
Sumac base with natural and dyed juncus on a grass bundle foundation
15.5 cm high
24.5 cm max. diameter
7 stitches per cm

85. **Storage Basket**
Yokuts type; ca. 1920
Bracken fern root and sough grass over a deer grass foundation
29 cm high
48 cm max. diameter
6 stitches per cm

83

84

85

86. **Basketry Bowl**
Yokuts type; ca. 1890
Willow; bracken fern; redbud
39 cm diameter
15 cm high
5 stitches per cm

87. **Basketry Jar**
Panamint type; ca. 1900
Willow, devil's claw, yucca root
9.75 cm high
14 cm max. width
15 stitches per cm

88. **Basketry Jar**
Owens Valley Paiute type; ca. 1910
Willow and devil's claw on a three rod foundation
10.5 cm high
13.5 cm max. diameter
10 stitches per cm

86

87

88

89

89. **Oval Gift Basket**
Pomo type; ca. 1890
Sedge and bulrush root on three willow rods; quail topknots; red feathers
15 cm max.length
5 cm high
14 stitches per cm

90

90. **Basket**
Pomo type; ca. 1890
Sedge and bulrush root on three willow rods; white glass beads; red feathers
16 cm diameter
9 cm high
11 stitches per cm

91

91. **Oval Gift Basket**
Pomo type; ca. 1880
Sedge and bulrush root on three willow rods; shell disk beads; white centered red pony beads; quail top knots; thread
33.5 cm max. length
10 cm high
9 stitches per cm

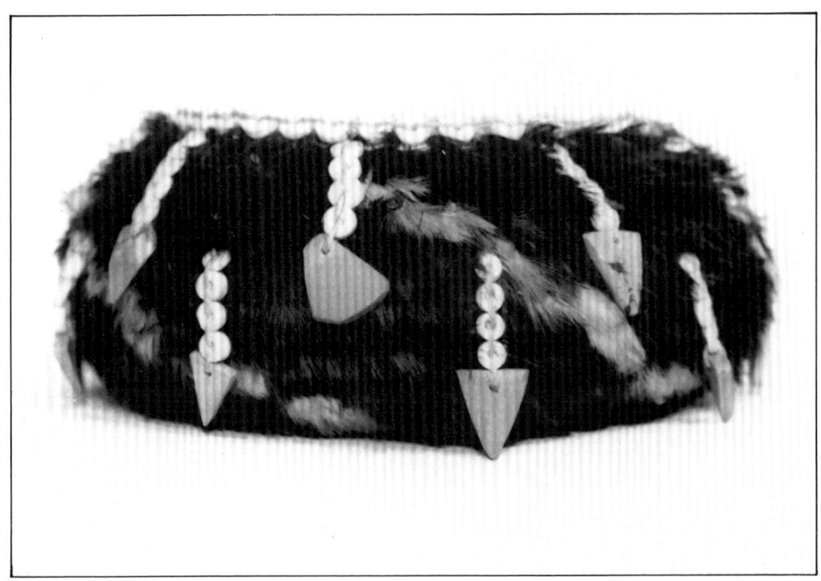

92

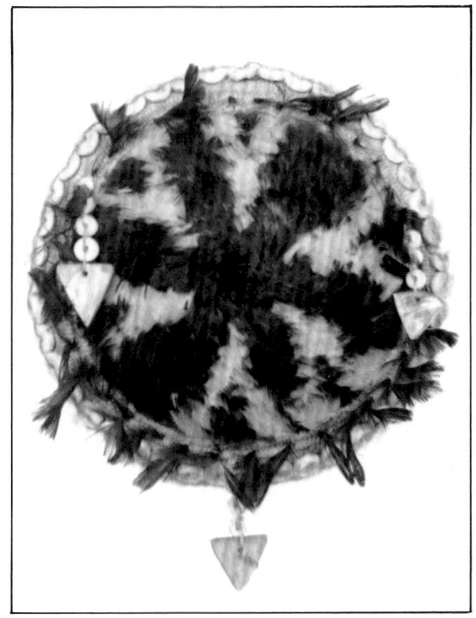

93

94

92. **Basket**
Pomo type; ca. 1890
Willow; clam shell; abalone pendant; hematite pendants; yellow meadow lark feathers; green mallard duck feathers
6 cm high
13 cm diameter

93. **Basketry Tray**
Pomo type; ca. 1890
Willow, clam shell; abalone pendants; yellow meadowlark feathers, green mallard duck feathers, brown quail topknots
10.5 cm diameter

94. **Oval Gift Basket**
Pomo type; ca. 1880
Sedge and bulrush root on three willow rods; shell disk beads; blue and white glass beads; quail topknots; red feathers (many restored)
44 cm x 21.5 cm
10 stitches per cm
There are two salmon pink flicker quills woven into the bottom of this basket.

Provenance:

Purchased at a Cape Cod, Mass. auction. Consigned by a local family whose relatives had been missionaries among the Pomo in the 19th century.

95

95. **Basketry Tray**
Tlingit type; ca. 1900
Spruce root; dyed bear grass in orange, yellow and purple-brown
33 cm diameter

96. **Moccasins**
Norway House Cree type; ca. 1900
Native tanned moosehide; fur lined; several shades of red, blue, green, purple, white and orange silk thread
26 cm x 8 cm

96

97. **Cornhusk Bag**
Nez Perce type; ca. 1890
Split corn husk; red, yellow, green, black, purple, grey, scarlet and orange worsted yarn
17 cm x 17.5 cm

Provenance:
Purchased at Robert W. Skinner American Indian Basketry auction on October 28, 1972. Lot 295. Catalog reads: "Nez Perce corn husk bag from area between Culdesac and Cottonwood, Idaho. Sa-to Collection."

98. **Beaded Bag**
Nez Perce type; ca. 1880
Canvas; red trade cloth; cotton fabric; leather strap; white, black, red, green, yellow, light, medium and dark blue glass beads
30 cm x 23 cm

99. **Storage Basket**
Twana (Skokomish) type; ca. 1880
Beargrass; cattail and cedar bark
33 cm high
34 cm diameter
5 stitches per cm

Provenance:
Amherst College collection. Inscription on basket says: 2975 Chilkoot basket.

97

98

99

100

100. **Figure**
Tlingit type; ca. 1880
Cedar wood; bone; native tanned leather; paint
15.3 cm high

101. **Basket**
Tlingit type; ca. 1900
Spruce root; dyed bear grass
15 cm high
17 cm diameter

102. **Rattle-top basket**
Tlingit type; ca. 1900
Spruce root; dyed beargrass in purple and orange; seeds or pebbles in rattle-top; cardboard reinforced bottom; signed on bottom: Mrs. Wilruut
9.5 cm high
14.5 cm diameter

101

103. **Beaver Bowl**
Northern Northwest Coast type;
ca. 1890
Cedar wood; abalone shell; white glass beads; opercula
40 cm long
13.5 cm high

104. **Model Totem Pole**
Haida type; ca. 1890
Cedar; red, black and blue paint
70 cm high

For another totem pole by the same hand see *Sotheby's Catalog No. 5096,* lot 328.

103

102

104

105

105. **Covered Basket**
Attu type; ca. 1900
Beach grass; metal or pebble rattle
20 cm high

106. **Sculpture**
Eskimo; ca. 1950
Black steatite
19 cm high
26 cm max. length

Provenance:
Tag on bottom of piece states: 36. Man Pulling Seal, black steatite, 5 x 8, East Hudson's Bay, Dr. John Parfitt collection.

106

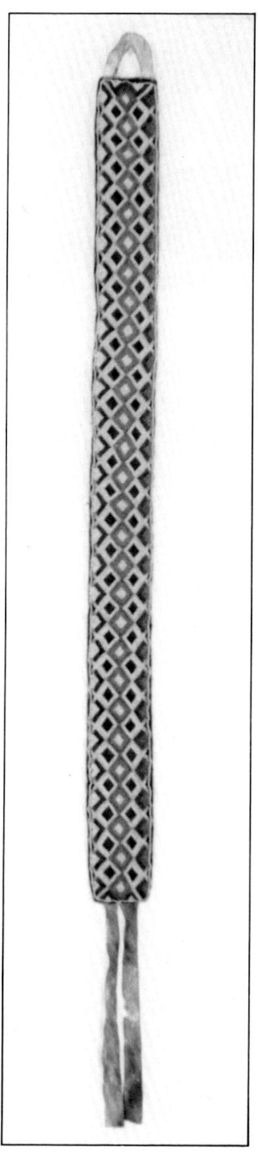

107

108

107. **Baby Belt**
Kutchin type; ca. 1905
Native tanned moosehide; velvet; cotton cloth; yellow, lavender, green, red, light, medium and dark blue glass beads
112 cm x 9 cm

For a similar example see Kate C. Duncan, *Northern Athapaskan Art,* p. 100, item 6.19. "Kutchin woman carrying her baby with a baby belt (Stuck 1916)."

108. **Covered Basket**
Attu type; ca. 1890
Beach grass; green, lavender and red wool
17 cm high

Bibliography and Footnotes

INTRODUCTION — CHARLES DERBY — PAGE 11

Bibliography

Mooney, James
1965 *The Ghost-Dance Religion*, Edited by Anthony F. C. Wallace, The University of Chicago Press, Chicago, Illinois.

Peterson, Harold
1976 *I Wear The Morning Star*, The Minneapolis Institute of The Arts, Minneapolis, Minnesota.

A UNIQUE "INDIAN" SHIRT — TED J. BRASSER — PAGE 15

Bibliography

Frisch, J. A.
1978 *Iroquois in the West. Handbook of North American Indians.* Volume 15. Smithsonian Institution, Washington.

Hough, F. B.
1853 *A History of St. Lawrence and Franklin Counties*, New York, Albany.

Speck, F. G.
1947 *Eastern Algonkian Block-Stamp Decoration: A New World Or An Acculturated Art.* The Archeological Society of New Jersey, Trenton.

FROM THE TOP OF HER HEAD: THE WOMAN'S DRESS CAP OF NORTHWESTERN CALIFORNIA — SARAH PEABODY TURNBAUGH — PAGE 17

References Cited

Bright, William
1978 Karok. *Handbook of North American Indians.* Vol. 8, *California*, edited by Robert Heiser (series editor William Sturtevant), pp. 180-189. Smithsonian Institution, Washington, D.C.

Eisenhart, Linda Lichliter
1981 Karok Basketry: Mrs. Phoebe Maddux and the Johnson Collection. Unpublished M.A. thesis, Department of Anthropology, George Washington University, Washington, D.C.

Elsasser, A.B.
1978 Basketry. *Handbook of North American Indians.* Vol. 8, *California*, edited by Robert Heizer (series editor William Sturtevant), pp. 626-641. Smithsonian Institution, Washington, D.C.

Fields, Virginia M.
1985 *The Hover Collection of Karuk Baskets.* Clarke Memorial Museum, Eureka, California.

Goddard, Pliny Earle
1903 Life and Culture of the Hupa. *University of California Publications in American Archaeology and Ethnology* 1 (1). Berkeley.

Harrington, John Peabody
1932 Tobacco Among the Karuk Indians of California. *Bureau of American Ethnology, Bulletin* 94. Smithsonian Institution, Washington, D.C.

Kroeber, Alfred L.
1905 Basket Designs of the Indians of Northwestern California. *University of California Publications in American Archaeology and Ethnology* 2 (4):105-164. Berkeley.

O'Neale, Lila M.
1932 Yurok and Karok Basket Weavers. *University of California Publications in American Archaeology and Ethnology* 32 (1):1-184. Berkeley.

Riverside Municipal Museum
1990 *Northern California Basketry.* Riverside Municipal Museum, Riverside, California.

Turnbaugh, Sarah Peabody
1977 The Anasazi Yucca Ring Basket. Unpublished M.S. thesis, Department of Textiles, University of Rhode Island, Kingston.

Turnbaugh, Sarah Peabody, and William A. Turnbaugh
1986 *Indian Baskets.* Schiffer Publishing, Ltd., West Chester, Pennsylvania, in collaboration with the Peabody Museum of Archaeology and Ethnology, Harvard University, Cambridge.
1987 Weaving the Woods: Tradition and Response in Southern New England Splint Basketry. In *A Key into the Language of Woodsplint Baskets*, edited by Ann McMullen and Russell G. Handsman, pp. 76-93. American Indian Archaeological Institute, Washington, Connecticut.

MICMAC PORCUPINE QUILLWORK IN THE DERBY COLLECTION — RUTH HOLMES WHITEHEAD — PAGE 21

Bibliography and Notes

1. See Whitehead, R. H. *Micmac Quillwork.* Halifax, The Nova Scotia Museum, 1982. Chapters 1-3. Portions of this essay were excerpted from Whitehead, R. H. "Micmac Porcupine Quillwork on Birchbark," in *Mohawk Micmac Maliseet and Other Souvenir Art from Victorian Canada: The June Bedford Collection.* Ed. June Bedford. London, June Bedford/Canada House, 1985:16-19.

2. Denys, Nicolas
1908 *The Description and Natural History of the Coast of North America (Acadia).* Trs. and ed. W. F. Ganong. Toronto, The Champlain Society, 448.

3. Robinson, J. and Rispin, T.
1944 "Journey Through Nova Scotia," in *Public Archives of Nova Scotia: Report of the Board of Trustees, 1944.* Halifax, Public Archives of Nova Scotia, 51.

4. Des Brisay, M. B.
1967 *History of the County of Lunenburg.* 3rd ed. Bridgewater, Bridgewater Bulletin, Ltd. 53.

5. The twelve boxes in the Derby Collection have been cataloged by the author from photographs only.

6. Charles Derby to R. H. Whitehead, personal communication, 11 Sept. 1989.

7. This reference to the Pictou woman is information collected from a published source by the author in 1980; the citation has been lost.

GREAT LAKES BANDOLIER BAGS IN THE DERBY COLLECTION — RICHARD POHRT JR. — PAGE 25

Bibliography

1973 *Art of the Great Lakes Indians*, Flint Institute of Arts, Flint, Michigan.

Fleming, Paula Richardson and Luskey, Judith
1988 *The North American Indian in Early Photographs*, Dorset Press.

Lanford, Benson
1986 "Great Lakes Woven Beadwork: An Introduction," *American Indian Art Magazine*, Volume 11, Number 3, Summer, pp. 62-67, 75.

Lanford, Benson
1984 "Winnebago Bandolier Bags," *American Indian Art Magazine*, Volume 9, Number 3, Summer, pp. 30-37.

Lessard, F. Dennis
1986 "Great Lakes Indian 'Loom' Beadwork," *American Indian Art Magazine*, Volume 11, Number 3, Summer, pp. 54-61, 68, 69.

Phillips, David R.
1973 *The West: An American Experience*, Regnery Co., Chicago.

Whiteford, Andrew H.
1986 "The Origins of Great Lakes Beaded Bandolier Bags," *American Indian Art Magazine*, Volume 11, Number 3, Summer, pp. 32-43.

Notes

1. The reader is advised to see "The Origins of Great Lakes Beaded Bandolier Bags" by Andrew Hunter Whiteford in *American Indian Art Magazine*, Summer, 1986, for illustrations of these two bags. The article also provides an excellent, in-depth discussion of the stylistic development of Great Lakes bandolier bags.

2. Benson Lanford's two important articles, "Great Lakes Woven Beadwork: An Introduction," *American Indian Art Magazine*, Summer, 1986, and "Winnebago Bandolier Bags," *American Indian Art Magazine*, Summer, 1984, each feature period photographs that illustrate this fashion.

3. Paula Richardson Fleming and Judith Luskey, *The North American Indian in Early Photographs* (Dorset Press, 1988) p. 199.

4. David R. Phillips, *The West: An American Experience* (Regnery Co., Chicago, 1973) p. 153.

A WICASAS SHIRT IN THE DERBY COLLECTION — F. DENNIS LESSARD — PAGE 27

Bibliography

Blish, Helen H.
1976 *A Pictograph History of the Oglala Sioux.* University of Nebraska Press, Lincoln.

Hassrick, Royal B.
1964 *The Sioux, Life and Customs of a Warrior Society.* University of Oklahoma Press, Norman.

Markoe, Glenn E., Ed.
1986 *Vestiges of a Proud Nation: The Ogden B. Read Northern Plains Indian Collection.* Burlington, VT.

Wissler, Clark
1912 "Societies and Ceremonial Associations of the Oglala Division of the Teton-Dakota," *Anthropological Papers of the American Museum of Natural History* Vol. XI, Part 1. New York.

THE ARCHETYPAL COLUMBIA RIVER PLATEAU CONTOUR BEADED BAG — JOHN M. GOGOL — PAGE 30

Bibliography

Anderson, Marcia and Kathy Hussey-Arntson
1986 Ojibwe Bandolier Bags in the Collection of the Minnesota Historical Society. *American Indian Art Magazine,* 11(4): 46-57.
Brasser, Ted. J.
1982 Pleasing the Spirits: Indian Art Around the Great Lakes. *Pleasing the Spirits, a Catalogue of A Collection of American Indian Art.* Ghylen Press, N.Y.
Conn, Richard
1986 *A Persistent Vision: Art of the Reservation Days,* The L. D. and Ruth Bax Collection of the Denver Art Museum. Denver Art Museum.
DeVoto, Bernard
1953 *The Journals of Lewis and Clark.* Houghton Mifflin. Cambridge.
Ewers, John C.
1963 Iroquois Indians in the Far West. *Montana, the Magazine of Western History,* 13(2): 2-10.
Gogol, John M.
1985 Columbia River/Plateau Indian Beadwork. *American Indian Basketry and Other Native Arts,* V(2): 4-28. Portland, OR.
Holm, Bill
1981 The Crow-Nez Perce Otterskin Bowcase-Quiver. *American Indian Art Magazine.* 6(4): 54-63.
Horse Capture, George P. and Richard A. Pohrt
1986 *Salish Indian Art From the J. R. Simplot Collection.* Buffalo Bill Historical Center. Cody, WY.
Lanford, Benson L.
1984 Winnebago Bandolier Bags. *American Indian Art Magazine,* 9(3): 30-37.
Lessard, Dennis
1980 Crow Indian Art: The Nez Perce connection. *American Indian Art Magazine.* 6(1): 54-63.
Porsche, Audrey
1987 *Yuto'keca: Transitions, The Burdick Collection.* State Historical Society of North Dakota. Bismarck.
Speck, Frank G.
1914 The Double-Curve Motive in Northeastern Algonkian Art. *Memoir 42, Anthropological Series, No. 1 Geological Survey of Canada.*
Walton, Ann T., John C. Ewers and Royal B. Hassrick
1985 *After the Buffalo Were Gone, The Louis Warren Hill, Sr., Collection of Indian Art.* Northwest Area Foundation. St. Paul, MN.
Whiteford, Andrew Hunter
1986 The Origins of Great Lake Bandolier Bags, *American Indian Art Magazine,* II(3): 32-43.

FIREBAGS OF THE FUR TRADE — TED J. BRASSER — PAGE 35

Bibliography

Peterson, J. and J. S. H. Brown, Editors
1985 *The New Peoples: Being and Becoming Metis in North America.* The University of Manitoba Press, Winnipeg.

APACHE DRESS IN THE DERBY COLLECTION — BENSON L. LANFORD — PAGE 40

Footnotes

1. Berlandier, Jean Louis, *The Indians of Texas in 1830,* Ed., intro., John C. Ewers, Smithsonian Institution, Washington, D.C., 1969. Paraphrased from p. 153.

2. HAIRPLATES are circular discs, usually of German silver or brass, which are worn either singly or in a long trailing row attached to the hair at the back of a man's head. They were in fashion among many Plains groups in the mid-1800s.

Bibliography

Berlandier, Jean Louis
1969 *The Indians of Texas in 1830* Ed., intro, John C. Ewers. Smithsonian Institution, Washington, D.C.
Ebert, Lieutenant James W.
1970 *Through the Country of the Comanche Indians in the Year 1845* Ed. John Galvin, John Howell Books, San Francisco
Ewers, John C.
1980 "Climate, Acculturation and Costume: A History of Women's Clothing Among the Southern Plains," *Plains Anthropologist Journal of the Plains Conference,* pp. 63-82.
Ferg, Alan
1987 "Western Apache Material Culture" *The Goodwin and Guenther Collections,* University of Arizona Press.
Hyde, George E.
1959 *Indians of the High Plains* University of Oklahoma Press.
Schneider, Mary Jane
1972 *A Museum Fellowship to Aid Museum and Field Research on Kiowa Beadwork* University of Missouri-Columbia, October.

A PIPE IN THE DERBY COLLECTION — BENSON L. LANFORD — PAGE 46

Footnotes

1. Dockstader, Frederick J. *Indian Art of the Americas,* Museum of the American Indian, Heye Foundation, New York, 1973, fig. 431.

2. Ewers, John C., editor, *Indian Art In Pipestone, George Catlin's Portfolio in the British Museum,* British Museum Publications Ltd. and Smithsonian Institution Press, City of Washington, 1979.

Bibliography

McCracken, Harold
1939 *George Catlin and the Old Frontier,* The Dial Press, New York.

A RARE APACHE MEDICINE BAG — JONATHAN BATKIN — PAGE 47

References cited:

Coe, Ralph T.
1976 *Sacred Circles: Two Thousand Years of North American Indian Art.* London: Arts Council of Great Britain.
Ferg, Alan, editor
1987 *Western Apache Material Culture: The Goodwin and Guenther Collections.* Tucson: The University of Arizona Press.
Fowler, Don D., and John F. Matley
1979 Material Culture of the Numa: The John Wesley Powell Collection, 1867-1880. *Smithsonian Contributions to Anthropology* 26. Washington, D.C.: Smithsonian Institution Press.
Morrow, Mable
1975 *Indian Rawhide: An American Folk Art.* Norman: University of Oklahoma Press.
Teit, James A.
1909 The Shuswap. *Memoirs of the American Museum of Natural History,* 4(7). New York.
1930 The Salishan Tribes of the Western Plateaus. Franz Boas, ed. Pp. 23-296 in *Forty-fifth Annual Report of the Bureau of American Ethnology to the Secretary of the Smithsonian Insitution, 1927-1928.* Washington, D.C.: Government Printing Office.

KIOWA BELT POUCHES IN THE DERBY COLLECTION — DAVID WOOLEY — PAGE 51

Footnotes

1. Early pony beaded shot bags (Kiowa/Comanche) usually of harness leather construction with a shoulder strap. An example in the Heye Foundation collections and also one in the Mount Holyoke Skinner Museum have surfaces which are fully backed.

2. For example, the Cheyenne child's belt with three strike-a-lights, numerous whetstone cases, awl cases, and charms illustrated in *Sacred Circles: Two Thousand Years of North American Art,* Nelson Gallery of Art, Atkins Museum of Fine Arts, Kansas City Missouri, by Ralph T. Coe, 1986, catalogue no. 475, p. 182.

3. Plate 21, Derby Collection. Note the Lakota doll with a belt with attached strike-a-light, knife sheath, and awl case.

4. For examples of females depicted in ledger drawings wearing belts with attached belt pouches see the following: 1988, *American Pictographic Images: Historical Works on Paper by the Plains Indian,* introduction and captions by Karen Daniels Peterson; the Henderson drawing book (Arapaho) Plate 71, woman with concho belt from which strike-a-light and awl case hang; 1987, *Kiowa Memories, Images from Indian Territory, 1880* Ronald McCoy, Morning Star Gallery, Plate 25, wives honoring warrior husbands and Plate 26, victory dance. Both drawings depict females with concho belts wearing strike-a-lights and awl cases.

5. For photographic examples of Kiowa and Comanche males carrying strike-a-lights, whetstone, or awl cases attached to bow and quiver cases, see *Plains Indian Raiders: The Final Phases of Warfare from the Arkansas to the Red River,* with original photographs by William S. Soule, Wilbur Sturtevant Nye, University of Oklahoma Press, 1967 including: Horseback a Comanche, p. 239; Horseback's Son, p. 241; Esa-Haney or Milky Way, p. 197; Gui-Tain or Heart of a Young Wolf, unidentified Kiowa, p. 225. For pictographic examples of Plains Indian males carrying strike-a-lights, or other pieces in ledger or sketchbooks see *Plains Indian Art from Fort Marion,* by Karen Daniels Peterson, University of Oklahoma Press, Norman, 1971, plate 52,

"okestcheimeme [Shave Head] and his best dress," by Shave Head, Cheyenne, May 21, 1875-April 11, 1878 p. 245, and plate 57. White Man, Ahsit, Cheyenne, p. 257. See also *Plains Indian Sketchbooks of Zo-Tom and Howling Wolf*, with introduction by Dorothy Dunn, Northland Press, Flagstaff, Arizona. The Cheyenne Howling Wolf, p. 51 is shown in a photograph with a bow case and quiver, with an attached strike-a-light.

For some comparative examples of Kiowa strike-a-lights, see 1987, Barbara A. Hart, Gregory C. Schwarz *Patterns of Life, Patterns of Art: The Rahr Collection of Native American Art.* Dartmouth College, Hanover, New Hampshire, distributed by University Press, Hanover and London, A Kiowa/Comanche strike-a-light catalogue no. 79, p. 54, collected in 1851. 1980, Barbara Hail, *Hau Kola! The Plains Indian Collection of the Haffenreffer Museum of Anthropology*, Haffenreffer Museum of Anthropology, Brown University (Kiowa Strike-a-Light catalogue #261, collected by Clark Chase near Fort Sill, Oklahoma in 1880). 1975, *The American Indian, The American Flag*, Flint Institute of Arts, catalogue 44, p. 50 (unusual strike-a-light with representation of an eagle). 1976, Richard Conn "Southern Plains Beadwork in the Fred Harvey Fine Arts Collection," in *Fred Harvey Fine Arts Collection, an Exhibition Organized by the Heard Museum*, the Heard Museum p. 82-85 (see Kiowa belt pouches, no. 86-87, p. 106-107. 1980, *Native American Art at the Philbrook*, Philbrook Art Center, Tulsa, Oklahoma (Kiowa strke-a-light catalogue #52, p. 36). 1989, Ann Lee Walters, *The Spirit of Native American Beauty and Mysticism in American Indian Art*, Chronicle Books, San Francisco, Colter Bay Indian Arts Museum (Kiowa strike-a-light with unusual curvilinear designs #255, p. 43).

Bibliography

Conn, Richard

1979 *Native American Art: In the Denver Art Museum*, Denver Art Museum, University of Washington Press, Seattle and London.

1976 "Southern Plains Beadwork in the Fred Harvey Fine Arts Collection" in *Fred Harvey Fine Arts Collection, An Exhibition Organized by the Heard Museum*, The Heard Museum, Phoenix, Arizona, 82-110.

Hail, Barbara

1983 *Hau Kola! The Plains Indian Collection of the Haffenreffer Museum of Anthropology*, Haffenreffer Museum of Anthropology, Brown University.

Holm, Bill

1985 "Old Photos Might Not Lie, But They Fib A Lot About Color!" in *American Indian Art Magazine*, Vol. 10, No. 4, Autumn: 44-49.

Mayhall, Mildred P.

1971 *The Kiowas*, University of Oklahoma Press, Norman.

Mishkin, Bernard

1940 *Rank and Warfare Among the Plains Indians*, University of Washington Press, Seattle.

Schneider, Mary Jane

1983 "The Production of Indian-Use and Souvenir Beadwork by Contemporary Indian Women," *Plains Anthropologist: Journal of the Plains Conference*, Vol. 28, August, No. 101: 235-245.

1983 "Kiowa and Comanche Baby Carriers," *Plains Anthropologist: Journal of the Plains Conference*, Vol. 28, November, No. 102, Part I: 305-314.

Wooley, David

1986 "Kiowa Historic Indian Art," an exhibition at the Plains Art Museum, Moorhead, Minnesota.

Acknowledgements

The Derby Collection contains some wonderful American Indian art objects. He is to be commended for making his collection available to scholars, collectors, and the general public. I want to thank Kathy Friese for her work in co-editing, and Sally Steffenson and Doug Deihl for their help in reviewing and editing this paper. Special thanks to Sharon Torkelsen for her encouragement and patience.

BELT POUCHES IN THE DERBY COLLECTION — BENSON L. LANFORD — PAGE 56

Bibliography

Hewitt, J. N. B. Editor

1970 *The Journal of Rudolph Friederich Kurz.* Reprinted by Bison Books, University of Nebraska Press. Lincoln.

Lanford, Benson L.

1980 "Parfleche and Crow Beadwork Designs," *American Indian Art Magazine*, Scottsdale, Arizona. Winter, Special Crow Issue, pp. 32-39.

Footnotes

1. Kurz, plate 26.

2. Bureau of American Ethnology negative number 3684-d, copied from an original print received from the estate of General Hugh Scott. It appears that this photograph was taken in Omaha, Nebraska in 1875.

AN IMPORTANT ACOMA WATER JAR — ROBERT BAUVER — PAGE 61

Footnotes

1. This pot, along with two others (Zias), were acquired in the spring or summer of 1891 from a trading post in Tiffany, Colorado, where they had been used as display items. The trading post was closing because the new railroad shop in Albuquerque had taken away their business. (Personal communication with George Baker.)

2. The term McCarty's has been used in labeling this time period. McCarty's is a small farming village of Acoma situated on land formerly claimed by Matthew McCarty, for whom it is named. Because the term may denote time period, provenance, or both, to avoid confusion it is currently less used.

3. Photographs by Ben Wittick, ca. 1882-85, Museum of New Mexico, Photo Archives, negative number 16034.

4. While the Acoma people view the entire jar as a unit of design with no smaller units recognized (Bunzel), we as analytical scholars feel the need to break them down into basic units to facilitate classification.

5. So it appears to me thus far, further research is required before this assumption can be verified.

6. Batkin, Jonathan. *Pottery of the Pueblos of New Mexico, 1770-1940.* (Colorado Springs, Colorado: Taylor Museum of the Colorado Springs Fine Arts Center, 1987): p. 147.

Bibliography

Bandelier, Adolph F.

1970 *The Southwestern Journals.* Albuquerque, New Mexico: University of New Mexico Press.

Batkin, Jonathan

1987 *Pottery of the Pueblos of New Mexico, 1700-1940.* Colorado Springs: Colorado: Taylor Museum of the Colorado Springs Fine Arts Center.

Bunzel, Ruth L.

1972 *The Pueblo Potter; A Study of Creative Imagination on Primitive Art.* New York: Dover Publications.

Dillingham, Rick

1977 "The Pottery of the Acoma Pueblo," *American Indian Art Magazine* Vol. 2, 4 (Autumn): 44-51.

Frank, Larry, and Francis H. Harlow

1974 *Historic Pottery of the Pueblo Indians, 1600-1880.* Boston: New York Graphic Society.

Harlow, Francis H.

1973 *Matte Paint Pottery of the Tewa, Keres and Zuni Pueblos.* Santa Fe: Museum of New Mexico.

Howard, Richard

1989 "How Old is that Acoma Pot?" *American Indian Art Magazine*, Vol. 12, no. 4 (Autumn): 46-49.

Stevenson, James

1883 *Illustrated Catalogue of the Collections Obtained from the Indians of New Mexico and Arizona in 1879.* Washington, DC: Government Printing Office.

MOCCASINS WITH HOLES IN THE SOLES — BENSON L. LANFORD — PAGE 86

Footnote

1. In writing about Mexican Kickapoo children, Ritzenthaler and Peterson state, "The baby's first pair of moccasins have tiny holes cut in the soles, as is the usual custom among the Central Algonkians. This is done so that, if the spirit of a deadman still wandering on earth invites the baby to come with him to the land of the dead, the baby can say, 'I can't make the journey. I have holes in my moccasins.'"

Bibliography

Ritzenthaler, Robert E. and Peterson, Frederick A.

1956 *The Mexican Kickapoo Indians*, Milwaukee Public Museum Publications in Anthropology, no. 2, page 57, Reprinted by Greenwood Reprinting 1970.

36 PIPE — CHARLES DERBY — PAGE 97

Bibliography

Ewers, John C.

1986 *Plains Indian Sculpture.* Smithsonian Institution Press, Washington, D.C.

Murie, James R.

1981 *Ceremonies of the Pawnee Part I: The Skiri.* edited by Douglas R. Parks, Smithsonian Contributions to Anthropology. 27, Washington, D.C.

Murie, James R.

1914 Pawnee Indian Societies, *Anthropological Papers of The American Museum of Natural History.* Vol. XI, Part VII, New York.

Paper, Jordan

1988 *Offering Smoke.* The University of Idaho Press, Moscow Idaho.

Weltfish, Gene

1965 *The Lost Universe.* Basic Books Inc., New York.